THE SERMON ON THE MOUNT

THE SERMON ON THE MOUNT

Meditations on Matthew 5:3 - 7:29

Fr. Anton P. Morgenroth, C.S.Sp.

TRINITY COMMUNICATIONS
MANASSAS, VIRGINIA 22110

ISBN 0-937495-19-0

Table of Contents

Introduction to the Beatitudes and the Sermon on the Mount

The Beatitudes speak to us of what it is to "follow Christ by loving as He loved", and thereby "to imitate God as children of His that He loves" (Eph. 5:1). They point to the indispensable demands and consequent blessings of redeemed life. And because they paint the perfection of *Christian* life, they describe and reflect the image of Christ (2 Cor. 3:18). The Beatitudes are the Kingdom of God come alive in men's hearts, "a kingdom of truth and life, . . . of holiness and grace,. . . of justice, love and peace" (Preface, Feast of Christ the King). They are the image, the mind of Christ coming to life in us, as God is "appealing through us" (2 Cor. 5:20). They are the manifold facets of that Love, which God *is* (1 Jn. 4:8 and 16), as He in that Humanity of the Eternal Word reveals "the glory that is His as the only Son of the Father" (Jn. 1:14). In the Beatitudes Our Lord reveals to us what it is to be like Him.

The Beatitudes describe Our Lord Jesus Christ. They remain incomprehensible unless they are seen in the light which He *is*—for He alone is "the light of the world" and without Him we do not possess "the light of life" (Jn. 8:12). If we want to know what "poverty of Spirit" is, we must look "to Jesus, the pioneer and perfecter of our faith" (Heb. 12:2). We learn from Him, Who remained "gentle and humble in heart", even while He "suffered outside the gate" and Whose degradation we are to share (Heb. 13:12-13). In Him we learn of the ultimate poverty of God Himself revealed in the emptying of Himself, the Son of God, even unto death on a Cross (Phil. 2:6-8). "Poverty of Spirit" points to Calvary, and Calvary illuminates the first Beatitude.

As the Old Testament prepares for Christ, for the Incarnation, for His life, His death and resurrection, the New Testament speaks of these mysteries as they came to unfold themselves, as they are further meditated upon and applied by the Apostles, as they were first lived, and opposed, in the young Church (Acts). This is the light by which "we see the light" (Ps. 36:9). The Beatitudes are perfections of God Himself, "Who has shone in our minds to radiate the light of the

7

knowledge of [His own] glory". And this glory is found "on the face of Christ" (2 Cor. 4:6). For whatever we see and hear of Christ reveals the Father Whom we can see and hear when we see and hear Jesus (Jn. 14:9).

As the words of the Gospel speak of Christ, the light which He alone *is*, can, if we "believe in the light", make us "become sons of light" (Jn. 12:36). Human words and concepts are taken from human life and experience. They are from below. Christ is from above, "Light from Light" (Creed), able to transfigure human words and human life into bearers of divine truths. Linguistic and cultural studies are helpful, but the Light which Christ was, is, and will be, is the Light by which "we see the light" and become light. We. who "were darkness once . . . now . . . are light in the Lord . . . children of light" (Eph. 5:8-9). "Anything illuminated turns into light" (verse 14).

The sacred, the created Humanity of the Lord became the vessel of heavenly, uncreated reality. This reality—God Himself, His will, His dispositions towards us—became visible in Jesus the Man, Whom to see is to see the Father (Jn. 14:9). His Humanity made Him visible "whose home is in inaccessible light" (1 Tm. 6:16). He in turn gives us, by the light, by the God-given power of faith, the ability to see divine reality and purpose in human, created language, action, appearance. This is so because "the Word", God in His Eternal Utterance, "was made flesh . . . lived among us, and we saw His glory . . . that is His as the only Son of the Father" (Jn. 1:14). It is the glory of the infinite God, Whose "two names, Being and Love, express ineffably the same divine Reality of Him Who has wished to make Himself known to us" (Credo of Pope Paul VI). God shines "in our minds to radiate the light of the knowledge of [His] glory, the glory on the face of Christ" (2 Cor. 4:6).

Meditating on the Beatitudes, delineating Christ-like life, is to meditate on Christ as He described Himself. Illuminated by the human life lived by the Son of God in His created Humanity, by the light shining into the darkness into which sin had thrown human history, thus illuminated, the Beatitudes become both a divine ideal and a divine possibility for men, divine reality coming to life in men. We become images of the Lord, "reflecting like mirrors the brightness of the Lord . . . as we are turned into the image that we reflect" (2 Cor. 3:18).

We seek God and His Will when we meditate on His word, when we seek the life of the Beatitudes. We are promised that we shall find (Mt. 7:7). But this "is the work of the Lord who is Spirit" (2 Cor. 3:18). As we begin to find, the human becomes transfigured into an image of the divine. Poverty of spirit will be seen as reflection of the "emptying" of Christ (Phil. 2: 6-8). Gentleness is seen as proclaimed by our Lord as

His (Mt. 11:29). Mourning is revelation of God in the tears of Christ shed over Jerusalem (Lk. 19:41-44).

Ideas taken from our experience will describe the divine in Jesus. He in turn, by His divine light, will illuminate the life described in human terms, divinizing our vision of the ideal and enabling us to grow into the life of the Beatitudes. This is possible since the Word had become flesh, had lived among us and enabled us to see in His Humanity the glory of God, that belonged to Him as the Son of the Father (Jn 1:14).

I

Beatitude

The First Beatitude

How blessed are the poor in spirit; theirs is the Kingdom of Heaven. (5:3)

The first Beatitude is both the foundation and perfection of the life of charity. It is the condition for the Kingdom of Heaven to be ours, and it is, in a world torn by sin and its devastating effects, the Kingdom of heaven possessing us. Poverty of spirit disposes us for transformation into the likeness of Christ, disposes us to follow Him, our "Way", that He may become our "Life", "Truth" and "Resurrection" (Jn. 14:9; 11:25). It is perfected by "meekness, suffering borne with patience, thirst after justice, mercy, purity of heart, will for peace" to ready us for "persecution suffered for the sake of justice" (Credo of Pope Paul VI). It has been the Royal Road for the Son of God, the road we are to follow, the road of the Son of God when He "emptied Himself" "being born in the likeness of man", "taking the form of a servant . . . [becoming] obedient unto death, even death on a cross" (Phil. 2:7-8).

Poverty of spirit is the foundation of the life of charity, of holiness, of union with God, of transformation into a likeness of Christ. It is that emptying of self by which room is made for the life of Christ in us—to "have been crucified with Christ" so that it is no longer I who live my own life (Gal. 2:19-20) of self-indulgence, self-seeking, self-assertion. Then Christ will be able to live in me. In the words of the Lord Who seeks to become our true life (Gal. 2:20), "if anyone wants to be a follower of Mine, let him renounce himself and take up *his* cross and follow *Me*" (Mt. 16:24). Poverty of spirit, as foundation of the spiritual life, is our readiness to trust God on the only road to Him, the road travelled by the Eternal Son, Who emptied Himself, not clinging "to His equality with God", even unto "death on a cross" (Phil. 2:6,8).

Poverty of spirit is readiness continually to make the transition from a life of self-indulgence, as described by St. Paul in its possible fruits (Gal. 5:19-20), to the life of the Spirit, that brings "love, joy, peace, patience, kindness, goodness, trustfulness, gentleness and self-control" (Gal. 5:22-23). But St. Paul reminds us that we "cannot belong to Christ Jesus unless [we] crucify all self-indulgent passions and desires" (Gal. 5:24). And this requires poverty of spirit—readiness to yield all to the demands of the Spirit. It is Christian readiness, even before the call for a specific readiness has gone out. This preliminary readiness—also a work of the Spirit—is at once answered by the demand to accept the Holy Spirit.

13

Poverty of spirit as *foundation* is obedience, is readiness to hear and do God's will. Poverty of spirit as *perfection* is the content of obedience. Thus the readiness of the Son of God—"here I am! I am coming to obey Your will" (Heb. 10-7—is brought to its perfection in His becoming "obedient unto death, even death on a cross" (Phil. 2:8). "Not as I will, but as Thou wilt" (Mt. 26:39). What He did, the circumstances of His life, His passion and death were the content, the perfection of His poverty, even unto total rejection by hate and rebellion of those whom He continued to love with the fidelity of God Who "is always faithful" though "we may be unfaithful" (2 Tim. 2:13). Rejection suffered in obedience, countered by redeeming love in obedience—this is the heart and source of all Redemption achieved for mankind.

"The glory on the face of Christ" radiating "the light of the knowledge of God's glory" may come to us through contact with holiness, in Christ-like people, in the life of the Church, in the beauty of nature or of art. It might awaken in us a profound discontent with ourselves, reveal to us the narrowness, the meanness of our ways, the rot in our hearts, the dwindling of our capacity to love, to understand. But the light enabling us to discover that we are on the road to spiritual death is also a light of hope, call to conversion, the discovery of God, even if He should remain hidden. As we remain faithful to the workings of divine grace, we will "come to consider all these [former] advantages as disadvantages" (Phil. 3:7). If the new Vision of a Love and Power that is from elsewhere is allowed to draw us on, and is finally seen to be the Lord Jesus Christ, Whom to see is to see the Father (Jn. 14:9) and Who draws all men to Himself (Jn. 12:32), we will become ready to accept the loss of our bonds of self-indulgence, and "to look on everything as so much rubbish if only [we] can have Christ" (Phil. 3:8). Truth, love, the beginning of resurrection have begun to prepare for the struggle between self-indulgence and the life of the spirit (Gal. 5:16-26). Poverty *of* spirit, *for* the spirit, detachment, self-control are seen to be necessary. Our helplessness on the new road to true life leads us to pray, to turn to Him Who is becoming our Light (Jn. 8:12) in which we see the light (Ps. 36:9), but also the darkness in our hearts. Free to reject the crosses which the new life finds in our struggle against sin, we can also always choose the cross and continue in our ascent to God, to eternal life.

This new thirst, the disillusionment with the vanities in life, the growing detestation of sin, the blessed vision of that peace which the world cannot give (Jn. 14:27), the glory of God that belongs to the only Son of the Father, now seen in the Word made flesh (Jn. 1,14), these constitute in us poverty of spirit, the foundation of growth of holiness. It is the necessary foundation for a life of the other Beatitudes, which are the perfection of the spirit of poverty—the realization of our helplessness and of the mercy and the power of God. And we will come to realize ever more deeply that "it is God, for His own loving purpose, Who puts both the will and the action into" us (Phil. 2:13). And then we will be ready to pray "Our Father".

The Second Beatitude

Blessed the gentle, they shall have the land for their heritage. (5:4)

While violence is growing in the homes, on the streets, in the world, in the media, the gentleness Christians must seek to acquire, the gentleness of Christ, is becoming increasingly "a sign that is rejected" (Lk. 2:34), a sign in growing contradiction to personal and public ruthlessness. The gentle become more and more "fools for the sake of Christ" (1 Cor. 4:10) to be written off and pushed aside. When they are cursed, they "answer with a blessing" instead of suing, when hounded "they put up with it", when insulted, they "answer politely", they are considered "the scum of the earth" (1 Cor. 4:12-13). It is the following of Him, Who, during that "hour. . . . [of] the reign of darkness" (Lk. 22:53) became "a thing despised and rejected by men, a man of sorrows" (Is. 53:2-3), ". . . . more worm than man, scorn of mankind, jest of the people" (Ps. 22:6).

But who among a people that demand conformity, who do violence to others by peer pressure, who are at the mercy of the media, who among us can find the courage to follow Christ Crucified—to live by the wisdom of God, which is foolishness to men (1 Cor. 1:21)? This is not only to be contradicted, but to become himself a "sign and instrument", a "sacrament" (Vatican II, *Dogmatic Constitution*, 1) of redeeming contradiction, sign of truth of Him, Who is "the Truth", instrument of Him Who is "the Life" (Jn. 14:6). Divine sign and instrument of revelation, Jesus Christ is the visible "image of the unseen God" (Col. 1:15), and we are called to be His followers. We *are* called "to imitate God, as children of His that He loves, and follow Christ by loving as He loved" (Eph. 5:1-2). And gentleness is part of His love.

The gentleness we are to practice as followers of Him from Whom we are to learn, *because* He "is gentle and humble in heart" (Mt. 11:29), has its origin in God. In a world that has fallen into contradiction to God, where truth and life are manipulated into lie and death, gentleness is necessary in defense against the onslaught of evil, and a necessary weapon against it. For evil in us is not eliminated in us by violence, but by conversion. That is why "the Son of Man has come to seek out and save what was lost" (Lk. 19:10). The Eternal Son, of infinite power, when He had assumed human nature, let Himself be arrested, condemned, humiliated, mocked and murdered. The ultimate of poverty of spirit was revealed in His obedience unto death, even on a cross (Phil. 2:8). Revealed were the humility of God, His human Heart, free of anger and resentment, and that gentleness without which the crushed reed may be broken (Mt. 12:20), the repentant sinner be driven away. For He came, the "beloved" of the Father, endowed with the spirit of the Father—"He will not brawl or shout, nor will anyone hear His voice in the street" (Mt. 12:18,19), as foretold by Isaiah. It is, in the translucent humanity of Jesus, a revelation of "the kindness and love of God our Savior for mankind" (Ti. 3:4) that the gentleness of the infinite God-Creator shines through. It is God's gentleness, God's pity that illuminates the gentleness and pity of Jesus. It will extend to us, to me, so that I, uplifted by His creative intention and power, may, in turn, be enabled to extend the gentleness of the Sacred Heart of Jesus towards others, and prepare the way for the transforming, creative gentleness of God.

The Beatitudes show what it is to be Christ-like, and therefore are descriptions of Christ. But to see Him is to see the Father, God, "whose home is in inaccessible light" (Tm. 6:16). At first the strictly human quality of gentleness is to be illuminated by the gentleness of Jesus, to be, as it were, interpreted by the divine light that shines *in* and *through* all His words, actions, sufferings. More light is derived if we see the gentleness of God not only in the Prophets, but in the God Who speaks through them. "I did forsake you for a brief moment, but with great love I will take you back. . . . I hid my face from you. But with everlasting love I have taken pity on you . . . my love for you will never leave you . . . says Yahweh Who takes pity on you" (Is. 54:7,8,10).

God's gentle love makes His mercy irresistible. It is the love of a mother. "Does a woman forget a baby at her breast, or fail to cherish the son of her womb? Yet even if these forget, I will never forget you" (Is. 49:15). It is the love of a father. "When he was still a long way off, his father saw him and was moved with pity. He ran to the boy . . . and kissed him tenderly" (Lk. 15:20). No reproach, only, "the rejoicing in heaven over one repentant sinner" (Lk. 15:7). Mercy in humility and gentleness gives to God's redeeming love a powerful attraction whenever it shines through. Who would resist Jesus' longing to gather Jerusalem's children "as a hen gathers her brood under her wings" (Lk. 13:34); or the prayer uttered in death agony for those, for us, who desired and brought about the murderous helplessness of the Crucified—"Father forgive them; they do not know what they are doing" (Lk. 23:34). One must fear that resistance to this love, infinite in power, yet gentle as a lamb, is close to final inpenitence. "Harshly dealt with, He bore it humbly . . . like a lamb that is brought to the slaughterhouse" (Is. 53:6-7). The "older son" was angry . . . and refused to go in to the banquet—and the banquet is a symbol of heaven. Was Our Lord telling us that this kind of hardness of heart excludes us from Heaven? We *are commanded* to love *as* Jesus loved (Jn. 13:34), "to imitate God, as children of His that He loves, and follow Christ by loving *as* He loved" (Eph. 5:1-2).

The "Land", the New Jerusalem, the Beatific Vision, will be ours only if we come to let ourselves be embraced by the gentle love of God, coming in the Sacred Heart of Jesus. For we are to learn from Him because He is gentle and humble in heart. His gentleness will pierce and heal our bruised hearts. And the embrace of Our Father, Father of ours, His prodigal children, will seal our salvation. Our prayer, "Come, Lord Jesus" (Rv. 22:20), however rarely prayed, has been heard. For God is "The Holy One in [our] midst, [He has] no wish to destroy" (Hos. 11:9).

The Third Beatitude

Blessed are those who mourn: they shall be comforted. (5:5)

Jesus' sadness in the Garden of Gethsemane is infinitely beyond comprehension. "My soul is sorrowful to the point of death" (Mt. 26:38). "His sweat fell to the ground like great drops of blood" (Lk. 22:44). His sadness contained that of all the broken hearts of all times. He became the Victim of all the sins that caused the immense sum of sadness that penetrates the world. This sadness He bore throughout His life on earth for He could not fail to sense and observe evil seeking its opportunity to strike men's hearts to make counterdisciples for the "prince of this world" (Jn. 14:30). The sadness of the Lord is a continuing presence, at every moment of His life, a continuous expiation, since He knew for every kind of suffering its source in the sins of men, in the sin of the world. It brought out the divine pity, because sin destroys the sinner, diminishes the spiritual level of the world, and crucifies others. Sin is refusal of the cross. But the refused cross must be freely borne somewhere, and this is expiation, the annihilation of evil by good (Rom. 12:21). Our Lord bore it all, since He is always the target of every sin—"in so far as you neglected to do this to one of the least of

these, you neglected to do it to me." (Mt. 25:45). "The words 'the insults of those who insult you fall on me' apply to Him", Jesus Christ
(Rom. 15:3).

When suffering becomes expiation, seen as the taking of a cross
rejected—rejected by me through my sin, by others through
theirs—every suffering becomes the birthpangs of new supernatural
life. "I must go through the pain of giving birth to you all over again, until Christ is formed in you" (Gal. 4:19). And when Our Lord likened the
sorrows His apostles were soon to suffer to the sufferings of "a woman
in childbirth" (Jn. 16:20-21), is there not a hint that their (our) sorrows,
if accepted, would extend the boundless expiation of Christ into history
and dispose others for Christ's sanctifying, creative expiation? Might it
be that unselfishness in suffering will become joy when its fruits become
known—in heaven? New birth to joy in pain: Is that not the law of true
life in a world that is permeated by rebellion against God?

It is a great grace to be saddened by one's own sins, sinfulness,
mediocrity, to be kept thereby from petrifying of the heart. When will
the closing words of Leon Bloy's *The Woman who was Poor* be realized
in me—"There is only one unhappiness . . . not to be one of the
Saints"? And yet, how much apparent sorrow for sins is largely sadness
for having failed, having been failing, not having satisfied one's vanity,
having caused loss, having made a fool of oneself.

What is this sadness, what are the sad mourning about? As already stated, if the Beatitudes describe Our Lord, He is the light by
which we *see* and *become* the light (Ps. 36:9). He is the source and the
model of what we are to be. His is supreme sadness, unrelieved from
the Agony in the Garden till His death. He sheds tears when seeing the
holy city, Jerusalem, and the Temple (Lk. 19:41-44), loved by Him with
deep intensity, foreseeing their total destruction, the horror of the mas-
sacre of His own people; the further scattering of the Jews across the
world; the aversion His people again and again would arouse among
Christians. For Christian antisemitism is largely the reversal of roles: we
should be victims of men's crimes and sins rather than making others
the victims of our lying accusations, making our scapegoats. Were the
tears shed by Our Lord reaching into the future? Tears shed over unspeakable sufferings deliberately inflicted, and over the destruction in
the hearts of the perpetrators.

"During His life on earth, He offered up prayers and entreaty,
aloud and in silent tears" (Heb. 5:7). How many nights, how many
hours? And all through His life? We cannot help assuming that His life
in Nazareth also knew frequent tears of entreaty and expiation. And is
it not likely that His Blessed Mother often wept silent tears for us in

that hidden expiation that was her apostolate?

Can we dare speak of sadness of the immutable God? Is joy in heaven (Lk. 15:7) pointing also to the possibility of sorrow? Is not the infinity of God, Whose names are Being and Love, the ground both for His immutability *and* for His inexhaustible flexibility in His relation with us? Do His power, justice, love and mercy not blend in the infinity of the Incomprehensible? Is sorrow confined to creatures?

Our most delicate and difficult task is to remain free of all resentment and self-righteousness when we meet with defects in the Church. Only if we remain free from pride, and allow ourselves to be profoundly wounded is it even safe to think about defects in the Church. If this sadness is not given us, it is better to leave the tragedies in the Church alone. Romano Guardini may have revealed a profound source of his own suffering, when in *The Church and the Catholic* he felt compelled to write: "The more deeply a man realizes what God is, the loftier his vision of Christ and His Kingdom, the more keenly will he suffer from the imperfection of the Church. That is the profound sorrow which lives in the souls of all great Christians ... Christ lives on in the Church, but Christ Crucified. One might almost venture to suggest that the defects of the Church are his Cross." And let us hope that we bear "one another's failings" (Gal. 6:2) in humility, "in fear and trembling" working for our salvation (Phil. 2:12).

The Fourth Beatitude

Blessed are those who hunger and thirst for holiness,
they shall have their fill. (5:6)

"God, you are my God, I am seeking you, my soul is thirsting for you. . . . Your love is better than life itself" (Ps. 63: 1,3). How often we would wish we could really pray and mean the words! "Seek and you will find" (Mt. 7:7). Have we really sought God and meant the words, "thy Kingdom come"? We cannot seek God, His Kingdom, His Holiness (Mt. 6:33) on our own terms, it must be on His terms, unconditional. And His terms are the two Beatitudes that describe the dispositions necessary for the Kingdom of Heaven—"poverty of spirit" and readiness to be "persecuted in the cause of right" (Mt. 5:3,10). To foresee the latter without presumption or paralyzing trepidation (if we were honest just once) is to live habitually in Hope—in ever deeper realization of our sin-induced helplessness (Jn. 15:5) accepted with an abiding sorrow for sin, but in humility and peace, "because God is greater than our conscience, and He knows everything" (1 Jn. 3:20). To live by the God-given power of Hope—paralyzed by sin, yet knowing that the Sacred Heart of Jesus longs to dispose us, like the paralytic in the Gospel, to receive absolution and be made to walk (Lk. 5:18-25) on our journey towards eternal joy.

Holiness is that union, that mutual indwelling with God into which we have been baptized (Mt. 28:19) and which is intended by God to deepen. It is the sharing "of the divine nature" (2 Pt. 1:4), the life-giving union likened to that of a vine and its branches (Jn. 15:5). Branches are to bear fruit: for us this means to be turned into true images of the Son (Rom. 8:29) by becoming like Jesus the Man, Whom to see is to see the Father (Jn. 14:9). It is to be the revelation and instrument of Christ, and thus *in, through*, and *as* the Church to manifest and actualize "the mystery of God's love for men" (Vatican II, *Pastoral Constitution on the Church*, 45).

Holiness is a gift from God, it is all grace. But it must be sought though the cost of being a seeker and follower of Christ may be heavy (Mt. 10:37-39). And it is the cost that makes us seek blessedness elsewhere. Life without the Beatitudes is easier, because the promises joined to each Beatitude, though fulfilled even now, remain hidden. Their fullness must wait till we reach eternal life. Technology has conditioned us to calculate and expect results *now*. Only by an intense spiritual life can we hope not to fall into the trap of applying technological patterns of thought to divine realities. For then the world of holiness remains closed to us, and there will never be a hunger and thirst for holiness. And if the satisfaction in my natural cravings is my goal and achievement, the words to the Church of Laodicea will be tragically verified in me: "You say to yourself, 'I am rich, I have made a fortune, and have everything I want', never realizing that you are wretchedly and pitiably poor, and blind and naked too" (Rv. 3:17). And is this not our tragedy?

How can we come to really hunger and thirst for holiness? Where do we discover this mysterious revelation? Can we do more than pray, "I believe, help my unbelief" (Mk. 9:24)?

Innumerable are the ways in which God is discovered. It all is grace, God's gratuitous gift, and *His* ways are above our ways, His thoughts above our thoughts (Is. 55:9). However to prepare the "rich soil" (Mt. 13:23) for the fruitful reception of God's word, two truths must be profoundly realized. Otherwise, false expectations, "the god of this world", will blind us "to stop [us] seeing the light shed by the Good News of the glory of Christ, who is the image of God" (2 Cor. 4:4).

First, we must seek to discern the wisdom of God, "the language of the cross . . . as God's power to save" (1 Cor. 1:18). We must discover that "God's foolishness is wiser than human wisdom, and God's weakness is stronger than human strength" (1 Cor. 1:25). "[One] must learn to be a fool before [one] really can be wise. Why? Because the wisdom of this world is foolishness to God" (1 Cor. 3:18). We may add, that the wisdom of today's world, by its bankruptcy, by its self-destructive madness, may point to another wisdom and where this true, divine wisdom is found—the Church.

Second, we can hardly discern God's truths without first beginning to see in faith the blending of His infinite power, knowledge and wisdom at the service of His mercy, of His redeeming love, together constituting His Providence. And, as the supreme Mystery of Divine Providence becomes the content of our faith, ground of our hope, invitation of our charity, we will be able to discern His beauty, His splendour, His glory reflected in holiness. The Holiness of Our Lord Jesus Christ will shine through those "more perfectly transformed into the image of Christ" so that in them, Jesus, and in Him, "God's presence and face" are revealed (*Dogmatic Constitution*, 50). The saints—above all, the millions of hidden saints in our very midst—"innocent and genuine, perfect children of God among a deceitful and underhand brood . . . shine in the world like bright stars" (Phil. 2:14-15). Conversion, daily renewed, will open our eyes to the traces of God in creation, and to the image of Christ, the presence and face of God, in the lives of the Saints. And if we are willing to seek, we shall find (Mt. 7:7) and the light of the holiness of God will call forth in us hunger and thirst for holiness. And we will begin to love because we know now that God has "loved us first" (1 Jn. 4:19) with a love that is gentle and of infinite power, jealous and forgiving, and faithful when we are unfaithful, "for he cannot disown his own self" (2 Tim. 2:13). For His name is Love.

The Fifth Beatitude

Blessed are the merciful: they shall have mercy shown them. (5:7)

"What proves that God loves us is that Christ died for us while we were still sinners" (Rom. 5:8)—that is, while we were hardened in opposition to God, hiding from Him, fleeing from His ever-present seeking *us* (Rv. 3:19). His mercy is His wisdom, a wisdom that is "foolish by human reckoning" (1 Cor. 1:27). "For God's foolishness is wiser than human wisdom, and God's weakness is stronger than human strength" (1 Cor. 1:25). It is by the folly of the Cross that the power of sin could be broken, that God, through the suffering Heart of Christ, could "show mercy to all mankind", having "imprisoned", having allowed them to be helplessly bound, "in their own disobedience" (Rom. 11:32). The blindness and paralysis of sin (Lk. 5:18) can only be broken and reversed by the creative, merciful love of God, a love that remains faithful though we are unfaithful (2 Tm. 2:13). And this redeeming love is the Father's response to the pleading of the Sacred Heart of His Son, Who, in Heaven, "is living . . . to intercede for all who come to God through Him" (Heb. 7:25). For did not He, the Son of Man, the Son of Mary, extend His merciful love to *all* men, to *all* His murderers, while they, while we, were succeeding in making Him, literally, the target and victim of our rejections? Did He not promise that, when lifted up from the earth on the Cross, He would draw *all* men to Himself (Jn. 12:32)? And as His rejected love went out to His enemies while He suffered men's enmities, He resisted evil and conquered it with good (Rom. 12:21).

"This is the Commandment He has given us, that anyone who loves God *must* also love his brother" (1 Jn. 4:21). It is unthinkable that we are ever justified in refusing to love where God loves. "Anyone not living a holy life and not loving his brother is no child of God's" (1 Jn. 3:10). But because loving others, *all* others, even one's enemies (Mt. 5:44), those seeking to destroy or harm us, is not easy, and without grace impossible, love of neighbor comes to us as commandment. In its ultimate form, it was given to us at the eve of His death, after washing the feet of the Apostles (Jn. 13:34). To love *as* Christ loved Who, in being tortured, mocked and murdered, would draw *all* men to Himself (Jn. 12:32)—all without exception. And neither are we to exclude anyone from our love. But what is this love?

Love is the name of God (1 Jn. 4:8,16), and therefore of that inaccessible light in which God dwells (1 Tm. 6:16), which God *is*. This love extends to all men in indefectible fidelity (2 Tm. 2:13), always seeking what is lost (Lk. 19:10). This the Father accomplishes through the human Heart of His Son, Jesus Christ, to whom all authority has been given (Mt. 28:19), the authority to *will* mercy, and to accomplish its healing effect by the divine creative power that is His as the eternal Son. For "in His body lives the fullness of divinity" (Col. 2:9). The infinite love of the triune God floods the Heart of Jesus in its capacity for divine love and life that had grown to inconceivable measure while resisting with merciful love His rejection suffered in torture and crucifixion. The ordeal of the passion and death ended, in the hidden mystery of His Heart, with the victory of mercy. And this mercy is to come *to* us and *through* us. For us, the mystery of redemption, of being redeemed, and the mystery of our call to the apostolate, are *one*. "A sanctity which sought its own, and made self its aim, would be a self-contradiction" (von Balthasar, *Therese of Lisieux*, p. xii). We are commanded to "be holy, for [God] is holy" (1 Pt. 1:16). To reject, to refuse obedience to these commandments is to reject God, to choose damnation.

We cannot hope to find mercy, without becoming channels of mercy. St. James paraphrases the Beatitude, leaving no doubt that salvation is cut off if mercy is refused: "there will be judgment without mercy for those who have not been merciful themselves; but the merciful need have no fear of judgment" (Jas. 2:13). The indescribable extent of the refusal of mercy among men, within families, in economic life, between peoples. within and between nations, is horrifying. Unless we knew in faith and hope that the compassion of the Heart of Jesus has the infinite creative power and wisdom of God at its disposal, we would have to despair. Rather, Christians should see in this a call to greater holiness, ready to become, with the Lord, "a sign that is rejected" (Lk. 2:34). I "must learn to be a fool before [I] really can be wise" (1 Cor. 3:18), with that foolishness of God that "is wiser than human wisdom" (1 Cor. 1:25).

God's love for us, in our situation of sin, is always merciful love. The extent of this mercy always reaches far beyond our rebellions (Rom. 5:20). His mercy had been tested when sin sought to destroy Him Whom to see is to see the Father (Jn. 14:9), Whom we violate and murder whenever we violate and murder each other. Nor is it necessary to kill to become guilty of murder: "To hate your brother is to be a murderer" (1 Jn. 3:15).

Mercy is mysterious because it is the name of God, and yet to be practiced by us. How can this be? How can we control what is hidden from us? As in all those manifestations of love that we are called to practice, it is our task to discern, in the light of faith and in following Christ, what merciful love demands. This we do in obedience to the New Commandment, to love as Christ loved (Jn. 13:34). The elevation of human acts of mercy, seen and done through grace, to the level of that charity that is "poured into our hearts by the Holy Spirit" (Rom. 5:5), will remain a mystery, hidden, beyond testing, above all certitude, a subject of hope. And we must remember that human mercy is not forgiveness by God, but only pointing to it, encouraging the sinner to seek divine absolution.

When we pray, "forgive us our trespasses, as we forgive those who trespass against us", we ask for that forgiveness that is initiated by the Heart of Jesus. If we, on our part, refuse to forgive, we tie the hands of God, Who alone "puts both the will and the action into [us]" (Phil. 2:13), as Christ was rendered helpless by three nails. It is in our power to damn ourselves. The world seems to be well on this road. And yet, we must continue to trust in Him Whose ways are as high above our ways and Whose thoughts are as high above our thoughts as the heavens are above the earth (Is. 55:9). "For the mountains may depart, and the hills be shaken, but my love for you will never leave you" (Is. 54:10). And while the sins of men finally seemed to achieve their goal, to remove God from the world, in His human Heart He prayed for those who crucified Him, for all of us, "Father, forgive them; they do not know what they are doing" (Lk. 23:34).

Kyrie eleison; Lord have mercy.

The Sixth Beatitude

Blessed are the pure in heart, for they shall see God. (5:8)

Pope Pius XI warned mankind over fifty years ago that not since the days of Noah has mankind known such a scale of evil. Since then we have seen the rise of Nazism and the spread of Communism, leaving incalculable wreckage everywhere in the world. We have seen the betrayal of much that Vatican II urged upon Christendom, which even the saintly Pope Paul VI could not prevent, though he and innumerable hidden saints among the faithful might have been instrumental in somewhat stemming the flood of treason and filth. Consider for a moment only the United States: legalization of the murder of the unborn at any stage of growth, the ever wider acceptance of hedonism as the American Way of Life, the teaching of error in many Catholic institutions, the widespread and seemingly naive acceptance of obscenities in dance and entertainment, not to mention the confusion among so many who are consecrated to the undivided service of the Church. However, we cannot evaluate the whole situation, since sanctity may well be flowering, but hidden, in God's own ways, according to His wisdom "that is wiser than human wisdom" (1 Cor. 1:25). But what we do see should urge the followers of Him Who was—and wishes to continue to be through us—"a sign that is rejected", increasingly to purify their hearts of "the things that make a man unclean", "murder, adultery, fornication, theft, perjury, slander' (Mt. 15:20, 19).

What makes a man unclean, makes him also blind to divine truth. If our thirst for life is absorbed by self-indulgence, "the opposite of the Spirit" (Gal. 6:17), if our capacity for God, for truth, for charity is filled with the fruits of self-seeking (see Gal. 6:19-20), we cannot "share the divine nature" nor "escape corruption in a world that is sunk in vice" (2

Pt. 1:4). And as we rationalize the lived lies which sins *are*, we close our-selves ever more to truth, to Him Who is the Truth (Jn. 14:6). We slide into the unreal world of lies, of fantasy, and become ever more unable to taste, to respond to, the truths of God, promised to the poor of spirit and to those who would rather be "persecuted in the cause of right" (Mt. 5:3,10) than betray the Lord. "People of immoral lives . . . adulter-ers, . . . thieves, usurers, drunkards, slanderers . . . will never inherit the kingdom of God" (1 Cor. 6:9-10).

Conversion alone can deliver us from the morass of vice. This will become increasingly difficult as our milieu grows in brutality, seductive ugliness, permissiveness, as the pressure of society to conform rather than to judge increases. Totalitarian possession of man can come as dic-tatorship of terror or as dictatorship of hedonism under the guise of compassionate atheistic humanism, hedonism being more seductive. "Many false prophets will arise; they will deceive many, and with the in-crease of lawlessness, love in most men will grow cold; but the man who stands firm to the end will be saved" (Mt. 24:11-13). Is that the way left to us, to stand firm? Yes, we must stand fearlessly seeking the unseen God in His visible image (Col. 1:15), as the Incarnate Word, for to see Him is to see the Father. We are assured that we will find if we seek (Mt. 7:7). We must wage a continual battle with the deceptions pressed upon us—often by people of apparent generosity, good will and charm. Only a determined, yet humble and often hidden, life of faith and medi-tation can bring about and deepen that purity of heart without which we are assured we cannot taste the hidden realities of God. *"Only* the light of faith and meditation on the Word of God can enable us to find everywhere and always the God 'in whom we live and exist' " (*Decree on the Apostolate of Lay People*, 4). It is to seek and entrust ourselves unconditionally to "that light of Christ which shines out visibly from the Church" (*Dogmatic Constitution*, 1), which is in turn "the universal sacrament"—sign and instrument—"of salvation, at once manifesting and actualizing the mystery of God's love for men" (*Pastoral Constitu-tion*, 45).

While the other Beatitudes describe Christian existence, Purity of Heart is also the way and the goal, the condition for that capacity for God which will always be filled as, in response to God's liberating gifts, this capacity expands. To see God face to face (1 Cor. 13,12) eternally is preceded in this life by the ability to "taste" God, the things of God, the will of God, the ways of God. That is why one "must learn to be a fool before [one] really can be wise" (1 Cor. 3:18), one must become at-tuned to "the foolishness of the message" that St. Paul preached when "he was preaching a crucified Christ" (1 Cor 1:21,22). The purity to taste God, to taste the divine enterprise in this life demands more than a conversion of the will—renunciation of the self and accepting the pattern of the Cross. It also, and first of all, demands rejection of human practicality in the realm of faith and fearless discovery of the "language of the cross . . . [to] see it as God's power to save" (1 Cor. 1:18). Purity of heart is a certain clarity of faith, in hope, and in the service of love, which achieves daily "the victory over the world" (1 Jn. 5:4). Purity of heart is the capacity for truth, for Him Who is Truth, Who in turn will burn away all lies, all fantasy, all illusion, all temptation urging us to live by these. And although our faith will be severely tried by our own weakness and by "the worries of this world and the lure of riches" which "choke the word" (Mt. 13:22), the truth that will make us free (Jn. 8:32) and deliver us from sin, lies and illusion will arrive in our minds and hearts.

While the other Beatitudes are instrumental in readying us for the Beatific Vision during the time we are fighting "the good fight of the faith" (1 Tim. 6:12), purity of heart is being built up now, while we are still "exiled from the Lord, going as we do by faith and not by sight" (2 Cor. 5:6-7). "Now we are seeing a dim reflection in a mirror" (1 Cor. 13:12). Now all the Beatitudes work together in our renewal by "spiritual revolution so that [we] can put on the new self that has been created in God's way, in goodness and holiness of truth" (Eph. 4:23-24). But we will be ready for the fullness of that new life, for eternal life, when we no longer depend on the light of faith to see "God's glory . . . on the face of Christ" (2 Cor. 4:6), when perfect purity of heart has made us fit for the beatific vision. Then "the ban will be lifted. The throne of God and of the Lamb will be in its place in the city; His servants will worship Him, they will see Him face to face, and His name will be written on their foreheads. It will never be night again and they will not need lamplight or sunlight, because the Lord God will be shining on them. They will reign for ever and ever" (Rv. 22:3-5).

The Seventh Beatitude

Blessed are the peacemakers: they shall be called sons of God. (5:9)

"The peace of God, which passes all understanding, will keep your hearts and your minds in Christ Jesus" (Phil. 4:7). This is a deep mystery, the peace of God which God *is*, the name of God, the peace which God alone can give. "Peace I bequeath to you, *my own peace* I give you, a peace the world cannot give, this is my gift to you" (Jn.

14:27). Words spoken perhaps less than one hour before all would begin to collapse—agony anticipating horror, and then the arrest, the beginning of the Sin of the World seeking to crush the Sacred Heart of the Son of God.

The peace Jesus brought was His victory over Sin which divides and destroys. Love sustained while being rejected is the bridge He built once and for all, when as target (Mt. 25:45) and victim of all sins of human history He was crucified by us, while His love for mankind, for each one of us, was maintained (Jn. 12:32; Lk. 23:34), enveloping us all in His provisional absolution. It is the actualization of God's mercy for all mankind (Rom. 11:32) in the broken Heart of Jesus. Since *all* sins enter into this rejection, tentative absolution could be given for *all* sins for *all* men. Reconciliation was made possible for *all*, redemption was achieved.

We do not have to look deeply into history to discover that among Christian peoples peace is not a characteristic of their mutual solutions. The Hundred Years' War, the Thirty Years' War, relations between Ireland and England, French-German relations, the tragic history of Poland—each war becomes even more savage and costly, and now even the "peace" between the great powers is due to mutual deterrent, or more clearly, to the maintenance of the threat of total mutual destruction, liable to draw all bystanders, all mankind into the disaster. Unbelievable, total blindness, stupidity, and then the apparent helplessness of those who would sacrifice their lives for real peace. Is Christianity, as we are assured by so many, merely fantasy, illusion, or cynical mockery of the growing numbers of victims of man's beastliness, selfishness, callousness and cruelty?

What can we discern as the pattern of history among Christian people? Was it not set by the One from Whom it all came? "*He* came to His own domain and *His own* people"—prepared by God for His coming for centuries—"did not accept Him" (Jn. 1:11). Did it not all end in torture, agony, crucifixion? Did not the Prince of Peace tell us that He had not "come to bring peace to the earth . . . but a sword", division (Mt. 10:34)? And yet, His birth has been associated with the angelic promise of "peace to men who enjoy His favor" (Lk. 2:14). Where is that peace? But then, did He not promise also His own peace, "a peace the world cannot give" (Jn. 14:27)? The "practical" wisdom of men, so successful and profitable (for some), peace built on manipulation and technique applied to human relation: its bankruptcy is seen everywhere "because the wisdom of this world is foolishness to God" (1 Cor. 3:18).

So we have to attune our minds to God's wisdom, we "must learn to be a fool before [we] really can be wise" (1 Cor. 3:18). Conversion of perspective is essential. Without it the victory of Christ will only be measured by that human wisdom which, perverted, unredeemed and blind, can never taste God's vision, "the foolishness of the message that we preach" (1 Cor. 1:21), "the language of the cross" (1 Cor. 1:18). "God's foolishness is wiser than human wisdom, and God's weakness is stronger than human strength".

On Calvary, human eyes could see only the victory of evil. But faith knows of the victory of love, invisibly dwelling and tested in the sacred, crucified Heart of the Savior. The essential, the true and lasting victory, was invisible then, and has remained invisible ever since. What really happened and continues to take place, the victory of God's love in the hearts of men, the hidden transformation of men's hearts, is the real building up of true peace, even here on earth, given to those who seek God, who seek truth, who long for the delivery from the prison of selfishness and sin for themselves and for *all* others.

Reconciliation with God has been achieved by the victory of Jesus' love while He suffered the massive rejection on the part of mankind. Invisibly, this love, this drawing of all men to Himself (Jn. 12:32), accomplished on Calvary, continues as the love in the human Heart of the Risen Jesus continues to go out to men, to "seek out and save what was lost" (Lk. 19:10). But his invisible flow of graces must be prepared for in men's hearts, must be seen by its fruit in those who have responded.

To prepare, to dispose the world for the peace of God, the peace of Christ, is the task of the Church, of each of us who, baptized into Christ (Gal. 3:27), *are* the Church. Jesus Christ made peace by the fidelity of His love, maintained, in obedience (Phil. 2:8) to the Father, for us who sought to destroy Him by crucifixion: but this total, all-embracing victory must become effective in the hearts of men, here and now, in history, in every place, at all times—it must be revealed by the Church Teaching in its source, the Cross. Its healing power must be actively extended into the discord among men, in the heart of man. The Church, in her members, must be ready to suffer the continuing opposition of sin, and to absorb it, as a historical, visible and invisible Cross—to "resist evil and conquer it with good" (Rom. 12:21). It is the extension of the Cross of Jesus Christ into every human, historical situation, where evil, horror, enmity is at work. The Christian, with St. Paul, must, in His "own body do what [He] can to make up all that has still to be undergone by Christ for the sake of His body, the Church" (Col. 1:24).

The pattern, already mentioned—"He came to His own domain and His own people did not accept Him" (Jn. 1:11), Who was "destined to be a sign that is rejected" (Lk. 2:34)—this pattern is completed by the redeeming love in His human Heart in response to the onslaught of evil. The opposition came from "His own people". In us, opposition also comes from our own heart, where all evil intentions originate (Mt. 15:19). Our battle is two-fold—against the evil in our heart, against opposition from without. Here lies our mission of peace, to seek and accept "the healing power of God's love" (Prayer after Communion, 21st Sunday) in our hearts, and to "make straight the way of the Lord" (Jn. 1:23) in us and around us, through prayer and expiation, by "setting our hearts on [God's] Kingdom first, and on His justice" (or holiness) (Mt. 6:33). Then we will become revelations and instruments of reconciliation.

"God in Christ was reconciling the world to Himself" (2 Cor. 5:19). "He has entrusted to us the news that we are reconciled", and we, the Church, in action and word are to proclaim this to all. "So we are ambassadors for Christ" (2 Cor. 5:20). We are to be "a voice that cries in the wilderness: make a straight way for the Lord" (Jn. 1:23). Like and with the Baptist we are forerunners, witnesses in word and deed, in love absorbing evil; we bearing "one another's burdens, and so fulfill the law of Christ" (Gal. 6:2), to carry into the world "the cross of our Lord Jesus Christ, through whom the world is crucified to [us] and [we] to the world" (Gal. 6:14). Thus we become peacemakers, sons of God, brothers of Christ Crucified, preparing the way for the Lord, and thus, as Church, "the universal sacrament of salvation, at once manifesting and actualizing the mystery of God's (healing, redeeming) love for men" (*Pastoral Constitution*, 45).

The Eighth Beatitude (1)

Blessed are those who are persecuted in the cause of right;
theirs is the Kingdom of Heaven. (5:10)

How sad we ought to be when we hear of the unspeakable sufferings men inflict on men, children of the eternal Father upon their brothers and sisters in Christ, and so often it all leaves us cold, our *compassion* apparently dead. Is it the beginning of that coldness which may well be a foretaste—or perhaps a warning—of Hell, when deadly selfishness and vices become absolute? How can we learn "to be sad with those in sorrow" (Rom. 12:15)? How can we share the vulnerability, the ability to suffer, and thus expiate, that was Christ's? "And sadness came over him, and great distress. Then he said to them, 'My soul is sorrowful to the point of death' " (Mt. 26:27).

His immense capacity to suffer, in soul and body, made it possible for Our Lord to be the target of all the sins of men, to suffer the sum of all rejections of God. For what we "neglected to do to . . . the least . . . [we] neglected to do" to Him (Mt. 25:45); these are sins of omission. All evil intended is ultimately done to God, Who, in the vulnerable humanity of the eternal Son could now be the target of rejection of God, suffering it all, expiring in agony, the Victim of the Sin of the World. And while the unthinkable—God being slain by men's sins—happened, He would, through and in His human Heart, "draw all men" to Himself (Jn. 12:32). Reconciliation of God and mankind was initiated and effected. The temporal, historical, visible victory of evil was at the same time the absorption of evil by the Love of the Sacred Heart of Jesus, Lord and Redeemer. "Obedient unto death, even death on a cross" (Phil. 2:8), "having loved His own who were in the world, He loved them to the end" (Jn. 13:1)—*therefore* God has highly exalted Him' (Phil. 2:9). His tested (Wis. 2) and victorious love became, by His death, irrevocably eternalized in His human Heart, to rise, ascend, and to be the source of redemption till the end of history, when God will be "all in all" (1 Cor. 15:28).

Blessed He Who was persecuted by all, crucified by us, because by His crucified love, He transformed the disaster of Calvary, the consummation of Sin, into a lasting victory, the source of all redemption, the Father giving Him "all authority in heaven and on earth" (Mt. 28:18) so He will in heaven, actively "draw all men to Himself" (Jn. 12:32). The victory of Calvary, of Good Friday, became through Easter "the power of the resurrection" (Phil. 3:10). Expiation under persecution has now become the soul and pattern of the true apostolate of the Church, which is "the universal sacrament of salvation, at once manifesting and actualizing the mystery of God's love for men" (*Pastoral Constitution*, 45), of the true life of the Church. But how am I to share in this apostolate? I may not be persecuted, or if I am made to suffer, it may well not be in the cause of the right. If the Kingdom of God belongs to those persecuted in the cause of the right, are we left out when we are not personally persecuted, or when our suffering is not in the cause of the right?

"There is daily pressure upon me of my anxiety for all the churches. Who is weak, and I am not weak? Who is made to fall, and I am not indignant" (2 Cor. 11:28-29)? If we could only enter the grief of the Lord, Who shed tears over the holy and beloved city of Jerusalem, His sadness revealing the mind of God. We cannot help hearing His words, "if you in your turn had only understood on this day the message of peace! But, alas, it is hidden from your eyes" (Lk. 19:42). If we would only share the anguish, the sorrow of Paul as he was aware of the blindness of his own people (Rom. 9:1-5), "their minds . . . dulled" (2 Cor. 3:14).

The Son of God, in becoming Man, "took to Himself descent of Abraham . . . to become completely like his brothers so that He could be a compassionate and trustworthy high priest of God's religion, able to atone for human sins" (Heb. 2:17). Are we, who are to acquire the mind of Christ (Phil. 2:5), not to seek and pray that we may share this compassion of the Son of Man? How can we be followers of Him Whose Sacred Heart, "bruised [by and] for our offenses, pierced with a lance, victim [of and] for our sins" became the salvation of those who trust in Him (Litany of the Sacred Heart). As "ambassadors for Christ" God could not appeal *through* us (2 Cor. 5:20) unless we begin to be wounded by the sufferings of others and by the destruction sin brings about in the hearts of sinners. We cannot remain interested onlookers, and make some calculated contribution "to feel good", fasting twice a week, paying tithes on all we have, as did the Pharisee who went to the Temple to pray (Lk. 18:11). Smugness, self-righteousness block even the omnipotent love from entering our hearts. We know the Woes uttered by Our Lord when confronting the self-righteous. "Serpents, brood of vipers, how can you escape being condemned to hell" (Mt. 23:33)? A last appeal of the Savior of all mankind!

The eighth beatitude can be ours by the divine gift of compassion, compassion for those who are victims of sin, of the enmity of sin, and for the sinners whose hearts suffer progressive destruction even to the damning of themselves eternally. For hardness of heart, callousness, blindness for the image and likeness of God in all men, for the call of all to become Christ-like, this acquired incapacity to recognize and respond to God's call, closing ourselves to any sort of compassion—it is the growing of Hell in the heart, and the danger of final impenitence (see Mt. 25:41-46; Lk. 16:19-31).

All persecution in the world, all injustice, all exploitation, all smugness and self-righteousness, all suffering should find a wounded resonance in our hearts. By the grace of God, we must be willing to share in the divine pity that fills the Heart of Our Lord and is extended into history, into this world, in the hearts of all who are capable and willing to suffer com-passion. It is the soul of expiation, it is the heart of the true apostolate—it is being sent, that is, entering into a new relationship, as forerunners and witnesses into the world, "perfect children of God among a deceitful and underhand brood . . . [to] shine in the world like bright stars" (Phil. 2:15). To face, to share vicariously this condition of the world without self-righteous indignation, to realize in sorrow and compunction my own enormous share in the Sin of the World that crucified the Lord, and continues crucifying Him in the Church and in mankind everywhere, is to be among those "persecuted in the cause of right". It should be a life-long sorrow accepted as expiation for my own sins and sickening mediocrity (Rv. 3:14-22). Without it, hope may become presumption. It may, however, by the grace of God, expand into a wider expiation. It should find expression when we pray those Psalms that are prayers coming from suffering hearts, uttered in the depth of suffering and persecution, now prayed by the Church in the Divine Office (such as Ps. 12, 17, 22, 31, 35, 38, 41, 42, 55, 57, 61, 79, 86, 88, 102, 120, 123, 140).

These prayers should be ours as we pray *for* and *as* the Church. It may well be a prayer for the gift of sharing the compassion of Jesus Christ, of His Mother, and of all the Angels and Saints. Then we might become true sisters and brothers of Him Who "suffered outside the gate to sanctify the people with His own blood." Then we might hear the divine call to go "to Him . . . outside the camp, and share His degradation. For there is no eternal city for us in this life but we look for one in the life to come" (Heb. 13:33).

The Eighth Beatitude (2)

Blessed are you when people abuse you and persecute you and speak all kinds of calumny against you on my account. Rejoice and be glad, for your reward will be great in heaven; this is how they persecuted the prophets before you. (5:11-12)

"As for the virtuous man who is poor, let us oppress him. . . . Let us lie in wait for the virtuous man, since he annoys us and opposes our way of life. . . . Let us test him with cruelty and with torture and thus explore this gentleness of his" (Wis. 2:10; 12:19). After speaking of persecution, Our Lord goes on to show the dynamic nature of evil. Abuse and calumny are meant to destroy the person in his dignity, to tear at the image and likeness of God in man (Gn. 1:27). The intention is not a goal requiring oppression or elimination simply as a means to an end. Our Lord seems to point to what is contained in the idea of hatred, the equivalent of murder, the undoing (if it were possible) of God's creation and likeness which man is—"to hate your brother is to be a murderer" (1 Jn. 3:15).

The prophetic words, fortelling the fate of Christ and of His followers found in Chapter 2 of the Book of Wisdom, reveal the diabolical, insatiable nature of evil, the hatred of God or of any reflection of His in creation, above all in man—virtue, intelligence, gentleness, justice, holiness, love in its many manifestations: the Beatitudes. It is the madness of the demons who would go out of the man possessed and request to be sent into the herd of swine, to lose even this abode when the herd "charged down the cliff into the lake and perished in the water." The neighbors would implore the Savior "to leave the neighborhood" (Mt. 8:31-34).

Hatred of God and of those attributes that can be shared by good men, will eventually turn into that iciness of heart that would perpetrate evil for the excitement found in sheer destruction and in provoking despair, in extending Hell among men here on earth. The methods of the Nazi holocost, the Gulags described by Solshenitsyn, all are prefigured by those leaders who, pleased with the total degradation of their Victim on the Cross "jeered at Him. 'He saved others', they said, 'let Him save Himself if He is the Christ of God, the Chosen One' " (Lk. 23:35). In Communism especially, as it is established over an ever-increasing part of the earth, we face something destructive, something utterly ruthless, a deep resentment of anything that would reflect the God Who is both "Being and Love, [which] express ineffably the same divine Reality of Him Who has wished to make Himself known to us, and Who dwelling in light inaccessible (1 Tm. 6:16) is in Himself above every name, above every thing and above every created intellect" (*Credo of the People of God*, Paul VI).

Evil is a dynamic, destructive force in the hearts of men, easily provoked to any excesses of violence, torture and lies. It is something Christ was bound to encounter, and which the Church, His followers, and all men of good will, are bound to meet. "If the world hates you"—and this means, seeks to destroy you and any remnant of the divine image in you, to murder you (1 Jn. 3:15)—"remember that it hated me before you . . . the servant is not greater than his master. If they persecuted Me, they will persecute you too" (Jn. 15:18,20). And this persecution comes not only from without the Church, but, as seen at present in the American Church, increasingly from within. When He came among His own, "His own people did not accept Him" (Jn. 1:11). The pattern was set then. It continues to this day and to the end of time, when "many false prophets will arise . . . when love in most men will grow cold" (Mt. 24:12). More than at other times it is necessary to recognize evil seeking destruction, evil directly intended, directed against God the Creator and Savior, and against His image, man. Recognizing and facing such evil, above all, if found within the Church, is a cross we must bear, in a spirit of prayer and expiation. We must hear the call, through it, to an ever more single-minded seeking of God and His holy Will. It is a call to humility, because it is a call to suffer persecution "in the cause of right" (Mt. 5:10), and this without self-righteousness. It is, "in fear and trembling" (Phil. 2:12), to expect extreme, murderous violence—and calumny is violence too—often under the guise of compassion, in the name of humanity. With St. Paul we will be seen as fools, although that it is "for the sake of Christ " (1 Cor. 4:10) must often remain hidden.

We are called to the real sharing of the cross of Christ, the instrument that was designed to draw all rejections of God throughout history upon the vulnerable humanity of the eternal Son of God (Heb. 10:5). And as He in His agony drew *all* man to Himself (Jn. 12:32), we are to channel this love of His into our own milieu and moment of history, "to make up all that has still to be undergone by Christ for the sake of His body, the Church" (Col. 1:24). It is "the cross of our Lord Jesus Christ, through whom the world is crucified to me, and I to the world" (Gal. 6:14). It is to be "crucified with Christ," like Christ; it is to be crucified by the evil intent to do away with God, with justice, truth and charity; it is to love as Christ loved—the New Commandment (Jn. 13:34)—so that I may live "with the life of Christ" (Gal. 2:19, 20). It is the ultimate, most bitter testing of our apostolate, with Christ, for Christ, like Christ, to "resist evil and conquer it with good" (Rom. 12:21). It is, in faith and apostolic love, to share God's desire for "everyone to be saved" (1 Tm. 2:4), to love *where* God loves and *as* God loves, now applied to my neighbor, though he may be my enemy (Mt. 5:43-48). We will thus become true "sons of the Most High . . . [Who] Himself is kind to the ungrateful and wicked." It is to be "compassionate as [our] Father is compassionate" (Lk. 6:35-36). It is to be a Christian, a follower of Him Who prayed, "Father, forgive them, they do not know what they are doing" (Lk. 23:34).

II

Witness

The Salt of the Earth

*You are the salt of the earth. But if the salt becomes tasteless,
what can make it salty again? It is good for nothing
and can only be thrown out to be trampled underfoot by men. (5:13)*

The possibility of the salt becoming tasteless was foreseen by Our Lord. And the Risen Lord Jesus did not confine Himself to the Church in Laodicea when He revealed to St. John about that Church: "I know all about you: how you are neither cold nor hot . . . but since you are neither, but only lukewarm, I will spit you out of my mouth" (Rev. 3: 14-16). And one cannot help wondering whether the Holy Spirit was involved in making the Church bringing before bishops and priests every year in the readings of the Breviary for twelve consecutive days the words of Ezekiel and of St. Augustine "On the Shepherds" (bishops and priests): "So let us see how the word of God, that flatters no one, addresses the shepherds who are feeding themselves, not the sheep" (Irish Breviary, Vol. III, p. 541).

What is a Catholic, a priest, a bishop to do when to him the content of the faith has turned into a great mountain of boredom? Has he lost the faith? Is it a trial to his faith to be lived through with unflinching fidelity, a night of the soul? Has the burden of a pagan milieu, of coping with unanswerable questions, human, scientific, religious, become too great? Who knows the heart of another man, when we do not even know our own?

Can we seriously wash our hands of any "salt becoming tasteless", of any crisis, of any discouragement, of any loss of balance, of any fatal overreaction in the life of bishop, priest, religious? Have we contributed by washing our hands, at times even in front of the crowd and saying, "I am innocent of this man's blood" (Mt. 27:24)? Have we remembered when tempted to self-righteousness, thanking God that we are not "like this tax collector here" (Lk. 18:11), that "love takes no pleasure in other people's sins but delights in the truth" (1 Cor. 13:6)? Have we made our own the great Prelude to the Hymn on the Paschal Mystery that speaks of the emptying of God the Son, becoming Man, that He may empty Himself further to "the condition of a servant", to suffer death,—"even to death on a cross" (Phil. 2:1-11)? Here we learn that even in our daily tasks we practice, and thereby learn of and acquire, the mind of Christ (Phil. 2:5) by being "united in [our] convictions and . . . love, with a common purpose and a common mind; . . . no competition ... no conceit ... to be self-effacing" while thinking of other people's interest (Phil.2:2-4). This is "charity" in our daily life, our daily attempt of "emptying ourselves", our daily cross (Lk. 9:23-26), our Way of the Cross while "being built into a house where God lives in the Spirit" (Eph. 2:18). It is to be "crucified with Christ", so that I can come to live "not with my own life but with the life of Christ who lives in me" (Gal. 2:19-20). It is my being fitted to the Cross, stretched in all directions, to "take [me] where [I] would rather not go" (Jn. 21:18).

Do we stand by each other when being taken "where we would rather not go", to be crucified like Peter, *with* Peter, the Vicar of Christ in our own time? Do we find, and give, support to each other, *in* the Church, *as* the Church, as "ambassadors for Christ . . . God . . . appealing through us" (2 Cor. 5:20)? If the salt—lay, religious, priest, bishop—becomes tasteless, do we not all share in the responsibility, in the failure when it happens? Have we been free of cowardice, of mediocrity, have we cultivated rich soil which alone provides understanding of the word of God (Mt. 13:23)? Or are we "blind men leading blind men" (Mt. 15:14), dragging each other into the pit of falsehood and rebellion, reinforcing each other, leading whole sections of the Church into schism or heresy, if not outright rejection of God?

Do we understand the terrible dilemma leaders of the Church at times find themselves in? They may be torn between the solemn obligation of protecting the faith of the faithful, while remaining representatives of Him Whom the Father had chosen and endowed with His Spirit to "proclaim the true faith to the nations"; Who "will not break the crushed reed, not put out the smoldering wick till he has led the truth to victory" (Mt. 11:18, 20). It is the dilemma between standing firm in protecting the faith of the faithful and at the same time keeping in mind the injunction of St. Paul, to "be kind to everyone, a good teacher and patient . . . to be gentle when he corrects people who dispute what he says, never forgetting that God may give them a change of mind so that they recognize the truth" (Tm. 2:24-25).

The problem is not new; it arose soon after the Resurrection. But already in the Epistle to the Galatians we have a stern warning against troublemakers wanting to change the Good News of Christ (Gal. 1:7): "If anyone preaches a version of the Good News different from the one you have already heard, he is to be condemned" (Gal. 1:9). Are we to please man or God? And what if error seems to be propagated with the intention—often quite obvious—to destroy the word, the way, the work of God?

Pope John Paul II has said: "In order to be a living sign of Jesus Christ in holiness of life, we bishops experience the need for personal conversion". And then, there is the right, the absolute right of the people to have answered "the cry that comes from every corner of the world: 'We wish to see Jesus' (Jn. 12:21). And the world wants to see Him in us". And yet, "the bishop is the sign of Christ's love for His priests . . . a sign of Christ's compassion".

Pastors of souls, bishops, the Pope, are to be salt, that gives flavor and preserves. They above all are called to manifest and actualize "the mystery of God's love for men" (*Pastoral Constitution*, 45), the mystery revealed in Him Who is "the Way, the Truth", "the Resurrection and the Life" (Jn. 14:6; 11:25). Only their readiness to suffer crucifixion can resolve the dilemma of protecting both the faithful and the shepherds who have lost the taste for the things of God.

Again, in the words of Pope John Paul II, "precisely because he cannot renounce the preaching of the cross, the bishop will be called upon over and over again to accept criticism and to admit failure in a consensus of doctrine acceptable to everyone. As a living sign of Christ, he must be with Christ a sign of fidelity and therefore a sign of contradiction."

"Bear one another's burden, and so fulfill the law of Christ" (Gal. 6:2).

The Light of the World

You are the light of the world. (5:14)

"God shows to men, in a vivid way, His presence and His face in the lives of those companions of ours in the human condition who are more perfectly transformed into the image of Christ (cf. 2 Cor. 3:18)" (*Dogmatic Constitution*, 50). "God's glory" is found "on the face of Christ" (2 Cor. 4:6). "To have seen [Jesus] is to have seen the Father" (Jn. 14:9). In Jesus there was seen a glory, "the glory that is His as the only Son of the Father, full of grace and truth" (Jn. 1:14). Jesus' humanity, living in indestructible union with the eternal Word—"true God from true God", visible "image of the invisible God" (Col. 1:15)—is "the light of the world" (Jn. 8:12).

"The Word", the Son, "was the true light that enlightens all men" (Jn. 1:9), filling His humanity with this light, for "in His body lives the fullness of divinity" (Col. 2:9). It is a "transfiguration" that once was allowed to break through (Mt. 17:2), but with the eyes of faith could always be seen in Jesus while on earth. Besides Mary and Joseph, the Shepherds saw it (Lk. 2:17-20), the Wise Men saw it (Mt. 2:11), and slowly, however imperfectly at first, it was perceived by His followers: "His teaching made a deep impression on the people because He taught them with authority" (Mt. 7:28-29).

The reality, the presence, the face of the invisible Father were revealed in the Incarnate Son, even, and above all, in the total "emptying" of the Word, when He became flesh and when He suffered crucifixion. It was the supreme revelation of the Name, of the very essence of God—Love—by total self-giving. But if Jesus could be the revelation of God "whose home is in inaccessible light" (1 Tm. 6:16), could we, even if we have to be raised "from the dust" and lifted "from the dunghill" (Ps. 113:7), become signs of God's presence and reveal His face? Can we reflect Him Who is "the light of the world" (Jn. 8:12), and become ourselves "light of the world", as we are here instructed?

The answer can only come from God. In the humanity of the eternal Son, where He was (and continues for ever to be) true Man, "He took to Himself descent from Abraham", for "it was essential that He should in this way become completely like His brothers" (Heb. 2:16-17). And speaking as Man, He could say, "to have seen Me is to have seen the Father" (Jn. 14:9). Of him St. John could say, "we saw His glory, the glory that is His as the only Son of the Father, full of grace and truth" (Jn. 1:14). However if Jesus the Man could be transparent to the invisible God (Col. 1:15), not by an impersonal instrumentality like a lens, but by transformation, by the transfiguration of His humanity, all human beings have this God-given capacity to "become true images of His Son" (Rom. 8:29). And this is not only a possibility, a capacity, but a goal set for all. We are all commanded to love each other as He, the Lord Jesus, loved us—it is the New Commandment (Jn. 13:34). "Love one another, as I have loved you" (Jn. 15:12). And how did He love us? "A man can have no greater love than to lay down his life for his friends" (John 15:13). And "what proves that God loves us is that Christ died for us while we were still sinners" (Rom. 5:8). And are we not all commanded to "love [our] enemies and pray for those who persecute [us]" (Mt. 5:44)? It is to love with the indiscriminate love of the Father (Mt. 5:43), an aspect of that God-given resemblance to our Father Whose sons we are meant to be (Mt. 5:45), and Whose perfection we thereby share (Mt. 5:48). It is the love of the Father which Jesus, the Son, shared and taught us when "He gave up His life for us" (1 Jn. 3:16).

This was the tradition ever since it has been taught by the Lord, ever since it has been sealed by the crucifixion, and renewed ever since by the martyrs. And it is the very form of Christian life, to be ready to be "persecuted in the cause of right", for the kingdom of heaven could not be ours without this readiness (Mt. 5:10). Without this readiness to suffer injustice rather than commit it we cannot be serious about the absolute priority of God. The great commandment, to love God with our whole being (Mk. 12:30), to have no other gods except Yahweh (Dt. 5:7), is to prefer death to sin, to lose one's life for Jesus' sake in order to find it (Mt. 16:25). "Try then, to imitate God, as children of His that He loves, and follow Christ by loving as He loved you, giving Himself up in our place as a fragrant offering and a sacrifice to God" (Eph. 5:1-2).

This growing hope and readiness for eternal life, a readiness that must be ours at the moment of death, is a readiness for God becoming "all in all" (1 Cor. 15:28), for eternal life. But how can I contribute to this transformation of mine, by which I am to become "light of the world"? The readiness is man's part in acquiring a capacity for God, which God will always fill. Though both readiness and capacity are grace, gift of God, the former requires more of a conscious cooperation on man's part, while it is God Who always "puts both the will and the action" into us (Phil. 2:13).

Faith enables us to discern what God wants, what He wants us to become and to be. This can be expressed in terms of virtues: faith, hope, charity, justice, fortitude, temperance and prudence, the gifts of the Holy Spirit. In Scripture we find further aspects of Christian existence (1 Cor. 13:4-7; Gal. 3:22; Col. 3:12-14; Phil. 2:1-4), dispositions that are accessible to our perception, in ourselves and in others, while the all-embracing source, charity, shares in the hiddenness of the mystery of God, since charity is the name of God (1 Jn. 4,8,16). These various dispositions are reflections of charity when charity is at work in concrete life situations, just as nature reflects in a limitless variety of shades of colors the source of all reflected light, the sun.

In faith we know of our eternal destiny, of the boundless love of God to which we are called to respond in love. "God's love for us was revealed when God sent into the world His only Son so that we could have life through Him; this is the love I mean: Not our love for God, but God's love for us when He sent His Son" (1 Jn. 4:10). "We are to love, then, because He loved us first" (1 Jn. 4:19). But our response is clothed in some of the many dispositions mentioned above. It is on their accessible level that we can discern what God demands, and then try to live—to think, to act, to repent—in accord with it. As we learn to love God "with all [our] mind" (Mk. 12:30), our intelligence, illuminated by faith, vitalized by hope, we will learn to discover God's will in the circumstances of our life, from moment to moment. Thus we acquire a capacity for the further influx of charity, though it will usually be hidden. For divine charity, transforming our lives, originates in God, flows though the Son into our hearts: "as the Father has loved me, so I have loved you . . . love one another as I have loved you" (Jn. 15:9,12). Our various dispositions, as expressions of love, are both the foundations of love and the perfections of love. They are, on our part, our readiness for love, our living in accord with love—foundations. They are transformed by virtue, by the power, by the fire of charity—"poured into our hearts by the Holy Spirit" (Rom. 5:5)—into a capacity for God, transforming us into a living likeness of Jesus, turning us into images of the Son (Rom. 8:29).

"And we, with our unveiled faces reflecting like mirrors the brightness of the Lord, all grow brighter and brighter as we are turned into the image that we reflect; this is the work of the Lord who is Spirit" (2 Cor. 3:18).

To Shine in the World Like Bright Stars

(You are the light of the world.)
A city built on a hill-top cannot be hidden.
No one lights a lamp to put it under a tub; they put it on the lampstand
where it shines for everyone in the house. In the same way,
your light must shine in the sight of men, so that seeing your good works,
they may give the praise to your Father in heaven. (5:14-16)

"Do all that has to be done without complaining and arguing and then you will be innocent and genuine, perfect children of God among a deceitful and underhand brood, and you will shine in the world like bright stars" (Phil. 2:14-15).

"Do all that has to be done", your duty, what you know to be God's will, as you pray daily that His will be done—and *then* to *complain* is to place yourself in opposition to God! And to argue about what is known, in faith, to be God's will is unequivocally to rebel against God. For are we not assured that God's "thoughts are not [our] thoughts, that [His] ways are not [our] ways" (Is. 55:8)? Can we really be serious in seeking the will of *God*—are we thinking of and listening to the living God, "the God and Father of our Lord Jesus Christ" (2 Cor. 1:3), "whose home is in inaccessible light" (1 Tm. 6:16), Whose motives are "impossible to penetrate", Whose methods impossible to understand (Rom. 11:33)—when we sit in judgment on His will, when we argue? We are speaking of the case when God's will is clear, not of the process of seeking His will.

"No one can be a Catholic without a simple faith, that what the Church declares in God's name, is God's word, and therefore true. A man must simply believe that the Church is the oracle of God" (Cardinal Newman, "Faith and Doubt", *Discourses addressed to Mixed Congregations*, p. 216). This holds both for dogmatic and moral declarations. And where these declarations, and their clear applications are concerned, we cannot question, we must not complain nor argue, if we try to become, to be, to remain "children of God" and "shine in the world like bright stars" (Phil. 2:15). Yes, it is not easy to be "light of the world", to have a steadfast will to follow Jesus Christ, to grow in holiness, to be "child of God" though surrounded by a "deceitful and underhand brood" (Phil 2:15).

We put our light "under a tub" if we refuse to see God's will; when we rationalize the truth away; when we accept "false teachers, who will insinuate their own disruptive views and disown the Master who purchased their freedom. They will destroy themselves quickly" (2 Pt. 2:1). We put our light "under a tub" when we "complain " and "argue", not in the pursuit of truth, but in our escape from truth, in our conversion against, away from God. "Though the light has come into the world" we may "prefer darkness to light because [our] deeds [are] evil. And indeed, everyone who does wrong hates the light and avoids it, for fear his actions should be exposed" (Jn. 3:19-20). Thus murder came into the world, when "Cain, who belonged to the Evil One . . . cut his brother's throat simply for this reason, that his own life was evil and his brother lived a good life" (1 Jn. 3:12). And are not envy, the resentment of intelligence, of beauty, of holiness the source of much persecution, especially as it arises within the Church? And is not the anti-intellectualism, making light of the content of the Faith, so common in the American Church, underlying much of the modernism rampant in our Church, a tragedy of incalculable destructiveness? As Abel became a judgment to Cain, the Prophets to Israel, Our Blessed Lord to the whole world—"a sign that is rejected" (Lk. 2:34)— the true followers of Our Lord will likewise suffer opposition. "A servant is not greater than his master. If they persecuted me, they will persecute you too" (Jn. 15:20). "A man's enemies will be those of his own household" (Mt. 10:36).

It is the solemn responsibility of those holding authority in the Church, members of the hierarchy, superiors in religious congregations, those in charge of educational establishments, to put the light "on a lampstand where it shines for everyone in the house" (Mt. 5:15). The "house" is the Church, and the Church is to "bring *all* men that light of Christ which shines out visibly from the Church" (*Dogmatic Con-*

stitution, 1). The massive failure of the Church of the United States, the persecution and neutralization of many of those who are orthodox, continues. We ought to read what Holy Scripture has to say, read it in all simplicity. Two examples must suffice here. "Your false teachers . . . will destroy themselves very quickly; but there will be many who copy their shameless behavior and the Way of Truth will be brought into disrepute on their account . . . but for them the Condemnation . . . is at work already, and Destruction is not asleep" (2 Pt. 2:1-3). "These people who only insult anything that they do not understand are not reasoning beings, but simply animals born to be caught and killed, and they will quite certainly destroy themselves by their work of destruction" (2 Pt. 2:12; see also Gal. 1:6-9). It would seem to be a situation that calls for great holiness in the Church, "to live by the truth and in love" (Eph. 4:15).

How do we become "children of light" (Eph. 5:9)? Is this "light" and intensive faith transforming our standards, expanding our grasp of reality, breaking through the veil of ignorance and of our persistent refusal of the light "for fear [our] actions should be exposed" (Jn. 3:20)? Is it faith to know of our "sluggish spirit, unseeing eyes and inattentive ears" (Rom. 11:8; Is. 29:10), and yet to hold on to the promise of God in Christ Jesus Who had come (and continues to call and to come in the Church) "to seek out and save what was lost" (Lk. 19:10)? If "the effects of light are seen in complete goodness and right living and truth" (Eph. 5:9), these effects became known in faith, their possibility in hope, and the realization of these effects becomes the foundation and fruit of charity. To be children of light is to live "by the truth and in love . . . [to grow] in all ways into Christ" (Eph. 4:15). Wherever this happens—the growth of new life, "hidden with Christ in God" (Col. 3:3)—"the body [of Christ] grows until it has built itself up, in love" (Eph. 4:16). The Church is further extended into the hearts of men.

Through the Church we are called, *into* the Church we are called, because we have been "baptized into Christ", we are "sons of God through faith in Christ Jesus" (Gal. 3:27,26). From now on, the Church increasingly "should be through us what she is for us. Christ should continue to be proclaimed through us and to appear through us" (Henri de Lubac, *The Splendor of the Church*, p. 161). "So we are ambassadors for Christ, God making His appeal through us" (2 Cor. 5:20). In becoming Christ-like, we become transparent to God, for we become like Him, Jesus the Man, the "only one mediator between God and mankind" (1 Tm. 2:5), Who is the visible "image of the invisible God" (Col. 1:15). "God shows to men, in a vivid way, His presence and His face in the lives of those companions of ours in the human condition who are more perfectly transformed into the image of Christ (cf. 2 Cor. 3:18)" (*Dogmatic Constitution*, 50).

If we "set our hearts on [God's] kingdom first, and on His holiness" (Mt. 6:33), seeking to *learn* of God's holiness and to *share* it (1 Pt. 1:16), we will be "exposed by the light [and] will be illuminated and anything illuminated turns into light" (Eph. 5:13-14). The source of the light we are to be is He Who is the Light of the World (Jn. 8:12). The veil that hides from us the truth, hides Him Who is the Truth (Jn. 14:6) "when the old covenant is being read" (2 Cor. 3:14), this veil Christ first must remove. "It will not be removed until [we] turn to the Lord" (2 Cor. 3:16). But once the veil is removed, "we, with our unveiled faces reflecting like mirrors the brightness of the Lord, all grow brighter and brighter as we are turned into the image that we reflect" (2 Cor 3:18).

"Anything illuminated turns into light. That is why it is said: Wake up from sleeping, rise from the dead, and Christ will shine on you" (Eph. 5:14). And then we will come to "shine in the world like bright stars", "perfect children of God" (Phil. 2:15).

III

Fulfillment

The Fulfillment of the Law

Do not imagine that I have come to abolish the Law or the Prophets.
I have come not to abolish but to complete. I tell you solemnly,
till heaven and earth disappear, not one dot, not one little stroke,
shall disappear from the Law until its purpose is achieved.
Therefore, the man who infringes even one of the least
of these commandments and teaches others to do the same
will be considered the least in the kingdom of heaven;
but the man who keeps them and teaches them will be considered great
in the kingdom of heaven. For I tell you, if your virtue
goes no deeper than that of the scribes and Pharisees,
you will never get into the kingdom of heaven. (5:17-20)

The fullness of "the Law and the Prophets" derives from their purpose, their goal—the Redemption of mankind, that the will of God, Who "wants everyone to be saved and reach full knowledge of the truth" (1 Tm. 2:4), be fulfilled. Certainly this Our Lord did not come to abolish, but "to complete" (Mt. 5:17). The *purpose* of the Law is to be achieved. As the study of vocabulary and grammar can cease when a new language has become a flexible medium of expression of truth, the simple prescriptions of the Law, having a largely pedagogical, formative function, can be discarded when that for which they prepared has arrived. Christ's entering upon His public life made what was preparatory superfluous.

However, the fundamental truths and consequent demands of the Old Testament remain. They are indispensable foundations of the New, of the full Gospel of Jesus Christ. Revelation of God in the history of Israel is revelation of eternal truth of and about God. The God of what to us seem contradictory dispositions—a *coincidentia oppositorum*—wrath and mercy, being immutable yet flexible, God Creator of the universe and the same God begging Israel to return to Him, in Whom mercy and justice have embraced (Ps. 85:10): it is the living God, "the God and Father of Our Lord Jesus Christ, a gentle Father and the God of all consolation" (2 Cor. 1:3). The God Whom in His own inspired words we ask for mercy in the Psalms (51, 130, and others) and innumerable other prayers of the Old Testament is the God Whose eternal Son became, as Man, the target and victim of men's sins, while remaining faithful to us, His murderers.

His death, resurrection, entering upon His Lordship in heaven

and the continuing sending of the Spirit of redeeming unity made possible the life of the Church, the life *as* Church—as members of Christ
Jesus now "seated at the right hand of the Father." Now His rejected
and victorious love goes out to all men. As on the Cross, He now, from
heaven, draws all men to Himself (Jn. 12:32). Now this love can and
must be proclaimed and become present and effective in the Holy Eucharist, and thus "the Church produces the Eucharist, but the Eucharist
also produces the Church" (Henri de Lubac, *The Splendor of the
Church*, p. 92). And so we are to *become* Church as *recipients* of Christ,
while thereby becoming more perfect *revelations* and *instruments*,
sacraments of Christ.

The goals of the history of salvation, from the Fall of Abraham, to
Moses, to David, and finally, in the immediate preparation of the Incarnation of God, to Mary immaculately conceived as the New Beginning from whose "flesh and blood came Christ Who is above all, God
forever blessed" (Rom. 9:5)—these intermediate goals must be proclaimed in all their truth and splendor. They must never be compro-
mised, diminished, no aspect hidden, "until [their] purpose is achieved"
(Mt. 5:18), for these goals were not only preparing for the Redeemer,
but also were constitutive of a lasting reality effective in the ongoing
history of redemption, the task of the Church seeking to reach and embrace all mankind. The great figures of the Old Testament affect the
continuation of what they were instrumental in bringing about in the
religion and life of the people from whose "flesh and blood came
Christ" (Rom. 9:5), Who forever will be "the glory of [His] people Israel" (Lk. 2:32). Like the Baptist, like St. Joseph as Protector of the
Church, like the Mother of Jesus as Mother of men redeemed and to be
redeemed on their long and heavy journey, like the Apostles,
"foundations" of the building which is the Church (Eph. 2:20), the
Prophets and the Patriarchs remain integral and productive elements,
now of the whole people of God. "The Church of Christ acknowledges
that in God's plan of salvation the beginning of her faith and election is
to be found in the patriarchs, Moses and the prophets. She professes
that all Christ's faithful, who as men of faith are sons of Abraham (Gal.
3:7), are included in the same patriarch's call and that the salvation of
the Church is mystically prefigured in the exodus of God's chosen people from the land of bondage. . . . Nor can she forget that she draws
nourishment from the good olive tree onto which the wild olive
branches of the Gentiles have been grafted (Rom. 11:17-24)"
(*Declaration on the Relation of the Church to Non-Christian Religions*,
4). The Law and the Prophets are lasting foundations of the New
Jerusalem, of Heaven.

It is a sad fact of history that even important aspects of the deposit of faith, of realities revealed, of the total content of the faith are often lost sight of. Again and again Saints were raised to remind of, to restore, what has (often conveniently) been forgotten. This is true with regard both to doctrine and to the application of the moral law. "The Church, clasping sinners to her bosom, at once holy and always in need of purification, follows constantly the path of penance and renewal" (*Dogmatic Constitution*, 8). Thus imbalances caused by Jansenism, deeply limiting and distorting thinking about God, very much alive today in the Church in the United States, are still unfinished tasks for the Church. Again, we always must watch out that economic or political injustices are not being rationalized by distortions of the content of our faith. How, for example, could the widespread anti-Semitism throughout Christendom, bloody and utterly horrid in its often murderous effects, have been maintained, if Catholics had read St. Paul, telling us that the Jews, "as the chosen people . . . are still loved by God, loved for the sake of their ancestors," that "God never takes back His gifts or revokes His choice" (Rom. 11:28-29)? One would have thought they had been told by their Shepherds of the great sorrow of Paul because of the blindness of his beloved people, his "own flesh and blood. They were adopted as sons, they were given glory and the covenants; . . . the promises were made to them. They are descended from the patriarchs and from their flesh and blood came Christ Who is above all, God forever blessed!" (Rom. 9:2-5). And did not the same enormous arrogance and hardness of heart of western man blind them into restoration of slavery and the slave trade for the New World? Where was the faith in Christ Crucified, crucified by me? Why was it so convenient to ignore the authoritative *Catechism of the Council of Trent*, published in 1565, where we read: "As our sins consigned Christ the Lord to the death of the cross, most certainly those who wallow in sin and iniquity crucify to themselves again the Son of God, as far as in them lies, and make a mockery of Him. This guilt seems more enormous in us than in the Jews, since according to the testimony of the same Apostle: 'If they had known it, they would never have crucified the Lord of glory' (1 Cor. 2:8), while we, on the contrary, professing to know Him, yet denying Him by our actions, seem in some sort to lay violent hands on Him" (p.57). But enough of this, perhaps the saddest chapter in the history of the Church, saddes because "anti-Semitism . . . is the most horrible blow yet suffered by Our Lord in His ever continuous Passion; it is the bloodiest and the most unforgivable because He receives it upon His Mother's face and at the hands of Christians" (Leon Bloy, *The Pilgrim of the Absolute*, p. 268). "In the sight of the city He shed tears over it," foreseeing its destruction, and because the city "did not recognize [their] opportunity when God offered it" (lk. 19:41-44). And it is the same Jesus, Son of God, Son of Mary, Who will come to judge the living and the dead. It may be wise to restore the Dies Irae to the Liturgy of the Dead. Why did Christians not weep with Jesus over the blindness of His people? Are they not blessed who mourn (Mt. 5:5)? Why did they, called "to share His degradation" (Heb. 13:13), inflict degradation on His brothers and sisters in the flesh?

The painful history of the Church teaches again and again how those infringing "even on the least of these commandments" and teaching them to others are to be considered "the least in the kingdom of heaven" (Mt. 5:19). In our day, how much easier it is to rationalize abortion, breaking the Fifth Commandment of the Law, even invoking compassion, when one has heard Catholic theologians proclaim that abortion is not always wrong. And where are the correcting voices of the Shepherds?

Truly, "heaven and earth will pass away, but [His] words will not pass away" (Mk. 13:31). That adherence to the word of God, to the Law of the Old Testament in its eternal purpose, man's redemption, to the words of the Redeemer, may require heroic faith is seen in history, both where such fidelity was practiced and where men failed through cowardice, weakness, ignorance, pride. No need to remind ourselves that this fidelity is violently challenged at present from within the Church, at least in the more affluent parts of the "free world." "Many false prophets will arise; they will deceive many, and with the increase of lawlessness, love in most men will grow cold; but the man who stands firm to the end will be saved" (Mt. 24:11-13). Not to let oneself be deceived is a matter of salvation, of escaping eternal damnation! But what of those who do not stand firm to the end? Can it be said that unless our "virtue goes no deeper than that of" Shepherds and Theologians, of so many people consecrated to the undivided service of the Church, and so visible, we "will never get into the kingdom of heaven" (Mt. 5:20)? We may well recall the injunction of St. Paul: "Work for your salvation in fear and trembling" (Phil. 2:12).

To Hate Your Brother Is to Be a Murderer

You have learned that our forefathers were told,
"Do not commit murder; anyone who commits murder must be brought
to judgment." But what I tell you is this: Anyone who nurses anger
against his brother must be brought to judgment. If he abuses his brother,

he must answer for it to the court; if he sneers at him, he will have
to answer for it in the fires of hell. (5:21-22 NEB)

"From the heart come evil intentions: murder, adultery, fornication, theft, perjury, slander" (Mt. 15:19). The intention shapes the quality, the character, the morality of what happens in freedom. Therefore, St. John could write: "To hate your brother is to be a murderer" (1 Jn. 3:15). To hate makes a person incompatible with the mind of God, Who "wants everyone to be saved" (1 Tm. 2:4). It is a disposition which compels God to exclude the one who hates from sharing His life. Therefore, "murderers" (in deed, by intention, by holding on to a disposition equivalent to murder) "do not have eternal life in them" (1 Jn. 3:15). Refusal to love where God loves, where Christ Jesus loves, breaks the New Commandment: "Just as I have loved you, you also must love one another" (Jn. 13:34; 15:12). He who hates separates himself from God Whose Name is Love (1 Jn. 4:8,16). But how can we come to murderous intentions, or their equivalent, is being shown by Our Lord in the words we are considering.

It is in the heart that murder is committed. A Christian becomes guilty of murder, when a human being, or a group or a class of men, are no longer seen, in faith, as images of God, as created, as willed by God. Presumably we cannot judge the heart: "man looks at the appearances but Yahweh looks at the heart" (1 Sm. 16:7)—presumably the Christian knows that we are all "baptized into Christ, have put on Christ" (Gal. 3:27), and that all distinctions among men have thereby been done away with. All men are called to baptism, and we cannot know whether or when baptism of desire has taken place. Here lies the foundation of man's equality, in our common destiny, God, in Jesus Christ, drawing *all* men to Himself (Jn. 12:32). Since Christ, there are "no more distinctions between Jew and Greek, slave and free, male and female" (Gal. 3:28). Here lies the mystery of true equality, which is not self-evident, as Jefferson wrote. Christ drew *all* men to Himself (Jn. 12:32), He shed His blood for *all* men (Consecration of the Mass; Mt. 26:28).

"Anyone who nurses anger against his brother" (Mt. 5:22) allows a spontaneous aversion, irritation, resentment to influence, to color his attitude towards another. Contrary to the Law, to the Commandment of Charity, he "takes ... pleasure in other peoples' sin" (1 Cor. 13:6) ... while charity "is always ready to hope" (1 Cor 13:7). He approves of his emotional reaction and feels somehow superior to others. He usurps what can only be done by God Who alone knows the heart of man. To nurse "anger against [a] brother" is to refuse to be reconciled, and with such a refusal we must not dare to approach the altar, since we obstruct in the heart what Sacrifice is meant to effect—reconciliation. It is to counter the Priestly Prayer of Jesus, "that they may be one as we are one" (Jn. 17:21-23). It is the beginning to want to *undo* Redemption, to undo the Cross. It is the beginning of our refusal to "be compassionate as [our] Father is compassionate" (Lk. 6:36). Therefore we are told not to judge, not to condemn. For in usurping this divine prerogative, we accept the primeval temptation, still alive in *all* of us *as* temptation, to "be like God" (Gn. 3:5). We thus live and judge by a lie, and fall more deeply into sin. We presume, we reject mercy, and "there will be judgment without mercy for those who have not been merciful themselves" (Jas. 2:13). To take pleasure in anger against a brother and to cultivate such anger is to cultivate self-righteousness, the only kind of sin that provoked the most frightening words from Our Lord: "Serpents, brood of vipers, how can you escape being condemned to hell?" (Mt. 23:33).

However we must realize that we cannot give up the duty to judge the actions of men. When we are told that we must not "be judgmental", frequently this means that we must not apply moral standards to what concerns us, to what goes on anywhere on earth. It would be to abdicate the power of the mind, instead of putting our God-given intelligence in the service of God, to "love God with all [our] mind" (Mk. 12:30). Judging, evaluating what goes on, what is proposed, is our sacred duty. Once a civilization frowns on moral judgment, evil will take over, and tyranny will replace justice. Tyranny rejects the rights of men, justice, the commandments, morality as revealed by God and applied by the Church. The State, History, these become the new gods and soon turn into "the disastrous abomination . . . set up in the Holy Place" (Mt. 24:15), with its death camps and its Gulags. The Christian who refuses to judge yet hopes that what he happens to dislike will somehow disappear from the hearts of men is not always in harmony with the Heart of the Redeemer: this is the optimism of the coward. Moreover if we abdicate moral judgment, we are "neither cold nor hot . . . [and] will be spit out of the . . . mouth" (Rv. 3:15-16) of the Lord Jesus Christ, we will become strangers to God. There is an infinite abyss between judging in truth and in love what is visible, and usurping the prerogative of God, now given to Jesus Christ, Who knows men's hearts and will come "to judge the living and the dead". Our Judge is now He Who is the target of all sins and Who has been their victim on Calvary. But He is the redeemer Who, on the Cross, drew *all* men to Himself (Jn. 12:32) and Whose crucified and victorious love continues to envelop us. We pray that His continuing seeing, judging, and drawing us would not compel Him to turn, at the moment of our death, to irrevocable judgment of condemnation, that we will not have to hear the words, "go away from Me, with your curse upon you, to the eternal fire prepared for the devil and his angels" (Mt. 25:41).

As anger continues its destructive work in our hearts, it will soon find expression in our outward behavior. Our loveless critique will poison our thinking, our speech, our surroundings. Abuse of the brother will soon follow, well rationalized, so that abuse will appear simply as due response to alleged destructive evil in the brother. Total reversal of the very core of Christianity is now achieved, justified by lies that will stifle the voice of conscience—the voice of truth, the voice of God. So far there is a pretense of objectivity: the brother is abused because he has become harmful, because what he *does* is considered destructive. The possibility of the brother's conversion is denied, extension of Christ's victory of love is no longer understood. There is no resisting of alleged evil, and conquering it with good (Rom. 12:21). The possibility of a Christian answer is no longer considered.

The final step is taken when the brother is declared and treated as evil in himself, and murder in its various forms appears now fully justified in the mind of the murderer. Now the sneer replaces former attempts to justify by rationalizing, and this involves shameless lying. Now the victim is simply declared of an inferior order, as the "natives" to be exploited were in the colonial days, and the Jews by the Nazis. Now all is permitted, even required. "Realpolitik" now takes genocide, holocausts for granted, like an extermination of vermin. Superiority of weapons, as in colonial times, or terror in dealing with the conquered is the way of keeping the executioner, the "master race" in power. Sneering is hatred at its coldest, most contemptuous. It is murder committed in the heart remaining as a permanent disposition.

The inventors and perpetrators, the rulers and major executives and executioners in this third stage, when the usurpation of absolute power does not even pretend to justification before a higher power, now enter upon the path of absolute corruption and self-damnation. Sneering, total disdain, disregard of anything human, destruction of any remnant of humanity—and the death camps, the Gulags will be kept busy.

This ultimate brutalization is not confined to the political sphere. It can be found in the intimacy of the family life, and wherever men form communities. Here we confront—and we threaten to revert to—the unredeemed condition, a continuing rejection of grace. We are in danger of becoming "immersed in this world, without hope and without God" (Eph. 2:12). We are liable to become slaves to passions and pleasures of every kind, our days passed in malice and envy, becoming odious ourselves, hating one another (Ti. 3:3).

And yet, all the horrors intended for and suffered by the myriads of victims—victims of genocide, of terrorism of governments, of ruthless and inescapable exploitation of slavery, of child abuse—were already suffered by Our Lord Jesus Christ, when he became the target and victim of all sins of all times in His Passion and on the Cross. And His response of love was meant for all, as on the cross He drew *all* men to Himself (Jn. 12:32). "However great the number of sins committed, grace was even greater" (Rom. 5:20).

"God has imprisoned all men in their own disobedience only to show mercy to all mankind. How rich are the depths of God—how deep His wisdom and knowledge—and how impossible to penetrate His motives or understand His method! . . . All that exists comes from Him; all is by Him and for Him. To Him be glory forever! Amen." (Rom. 11, 33, 36).

"God's foolishness is wiser than human wisdom, and God's weakness is stronger than human strength" (1 Cor. 1:25). Yes, hope remains open till the moment of death (2 Tm. 2:13).

"Father, forgive them; they do not know what they are doing" (Lk. 23:34).

Judgment Without Mercy for the Merciless

So then, if you are bringing your offering to the altar
and there remember that your brother has something against you,
leave your offering there before the altar, go and be reconciled
with your brother first, and then come back and present your offering.
Come to terms with your opponent in good time while you are still
on the way to the court with him, or he may hand you over to the judge
and the judge to the officer, and you will be thrown into prison. I tell you
solemnly, you will not get out till you have paid the last penny. (5:23-26)

Although the Eucharist and the preparatory Sacrament of Penance and Reconciliation did not yet exist when Our Lord spoke these words, they clearly deal with situations often so painfully present in our lives. We seek union with Jesus Christ in and through His cross, through the victory of His love achieved during the Passion and Crucifixion. This means that we want reconciliation, peace on earth, but we really do not wish to have any share whatever in the cross of Jesus Christ; we do not want to obey the commandment to love as He loved all men, His executioners. We do not want to love our enemies, as commanded (Mt. 5:44). We do not want to pay this price to become "sons of [Our] Father in heaven" (Mt. 5:45), to share this perfection of the heavenly Father (Mt. 5:48).

But Our Lord's words were not options, counsels of perfection. If Jesus is the Savior, if He is the Way (Jn. 14:6), our salvation is not found elsewhere. And there is only *one* alternative to salvation, to the Way of the Cross—to hear His words: "Go away from Me, with your curse upon you, to the eternal fire prepared for the devil and his angels" (Mt. 25:41). For in refusing to love *where* and *as* Jesus loves, directing the love of the eternal Father towards *all* men, we have become incompatible with Him Who is Creator of all, Who sustains "the universe by His powerful command" (Heb. 1:3), Who is Our Savior, "a gentle Father and the God of all consolation" (2 Cor. 1:3). Refusing to seek reconciliation with our fellow man we oppose God Who "wants everyone to be saved" (1 Tim. 2:4).

If the words of Our Lord are applied to celebrating Mass—"if you are bringing you offering to the altar"—the contrast between our disposition of refusing or neglecting or postponing reconciliation and the reality of the Mass is even sharper than it would have been in the Old Testament sacrifice. Our Lord would soon teach that we must love our enemies, that is, desire, pray and labor for their ultimate good, conversion and salvation. This involves not only readiness for reconciliation, but a strong, even burning desire. But how is this humanly possible? The truth is that it is not; only grace can dispose us for it. Only the God-given power of hope for the other, for the enemy, rooted in the reality we know by faith of God's love and fidelity in love, can support us in acting contrary to our feelings and destructive inclinations, in contradiction to all pressures of society. Only as we begin to grasp how we are redeemed—by the fidelity of the Love of God in the Sacred human Heart of Jesus—can we become constructive, be forerunners of the Redeemer, prepare the way of grace.

Perhaps we ought to think of the Seven Last Words of Jesus to realize that refusal to be reconciled cannot be maintained while trying to be a follower of the One Who spoke, meant, lived, flawlessly *was*, these Seven Words, having come to the end of emptying Himself, "obedient unto death, even death on a cross" (Phil. 2:8). He Whose name is Love is being rejected by man, by mankind; He is the target of every rejection, from Adam to the end of time, when "love in most men will grow cold" (Mt. 24:12). And now, Victim of this massive rejection, crushed by man's rebellion, which forms so much of the history of mankind, it is now played out in Gulags covering the whole earth, not only those of the Soviet Union. The intention of the Gulags finds it way into the air-conditioned homes of the affluent, who do not want to realize that they too are brutalized and brutalizing victims of sin, that they too must choose between being crucified or being engaged in crucifying. We can no longer escape the cross. We are either Victim or Executioner.

The love of the Creator, Whose name is Love, rendered helpless by man's ongoing rebellion, in inconceivable struggle upholding His love for His torturers and murderers, pleads: "Father, forgive them; they do not know what they are doing" (Lk. 23:34). The love that made him create the universe that man might inhabit and behold it here pleads in agony for us who ignore and reject His love, Him Who is Love. Now, "a worm and no man" (Ps. 22:6), yet He is the Lord, Who, "in overflowing wrath for a moment" hid his face from us, but with everlasting love . . . will have compassion on [us], . . . the Lord, [Our] Redeemer" (Is. 54:8).

"I promise you, today you will be with Me in paradise" (Lk. 23:43). This promise can become one directed to me if, like the Good Thief, I cry out to the Lord "from the depth" of the prison of my selfishness, confusion, acquired paralysis of my conscience, of my mediocrity, being "neither cold nor hot," to be spit out of His mouth (Rv. 3:15-16). When will I learn to mean what I say: "Lord, have mercy," "forgive us our trespasses," "pray for us sinners," "Lord, listen to my cry for help" (Ps. 130:2), "have mercy on me . . . having sinned against no other than You" (Ps. 51:1,4)? When will my guilt feelings no longer be expressions of sadness for having made a fool of myself, having lost my self-esteem, but rather because I have slighted, rejected, ignored the love of God Who, in His humanity, wept for me (Lk. 19:4), Who "during His life on earth . . . offered up prayer and entreaty, aloud and in silent tears" (Heb. 5:7)?

When will I realize that I have become, by the creative word of Jesus, by the decision of His Sacred Heart and the transforming power of His deity, a son or daughter of His Mother? "Then to the disciple He said, 'This is your Mother' "(Jn. 19:27). When will I learn that she, that her memory, that her continuing tasks of drawing all men to her Son that He might be born in the hearts of men, is also entrusted to me, her child? That her birthpangs, suffered under the cross, are now to become continuing historical reality in me? That her apostolic universal task, as Church in perfection, and constitutive of the continuing Motherhood of the Church, is now to extend through me, as revelation and instrument of her Motherhood? She is my mother, I her child, to become Jesus" "brother and sister and mother," as anyone does who "does the will of [His] father in heaven" (Mt. 12:50). "Woman, this is your son" (Jn. 19:26).

May we dare to conjecture that the rejections of God throughout history, taking their course against Jesus in His crucifixion, were allowed to bring the Lord to experience what Sin brings about? As Jesus became the target and victim of the Sin of the World, He suffered what Sin intends. But He does not yet suffer the destruction sin brings about in the sinner, that makes the sinner incompatible with truth, with love, with God, makes him unfit for God, diminishes and even destroys his capacity for God. The sinner tumbles into alienation from the very source of his being, from the goal for which he was created, to which he has been called—God, his Creator and Redeemer. Rebellion against God is ultimate distortion, ultimate lie, ultimate isolation—"to stop loving, to stop understanding—and yet to live" (George Bernanos, *Diary of a Country Priest*, p. 163).

Our Lord had to be more than the victim of Sin. He had to suffer being torn from God, to experience, not as a tourist, but in real solidarity with those damning themselves, the spiritual suicide desertion from God brings about. For Him, Who could not sin, it meant desertion *by* God without consolation. Could that point to the mystery of His cry, "My God, My God, why have You deserted Me?" (Mt. 27:46)?

We discover ever new facets of God's love. We hear Jesus' cry, "I thirst" (Jn. 19:28). Is His thirst pointing to a deeper thirst, for the conversion and salvation of His murderers, of men through the ages? Are these thirsts not rather divergent? Thirst inflicted by the sadism of His murderers, countered by His thirst, a spectacle to be mocked, while Jesus' love would absorb malice in the hidden recesses of His Heart, the love which, in the torn Heart of the Savior, would, in desperate struggle, be maintained in obedience to the Father. It is the Father's love filling the human Heart of Jesus. "With everlasting love I have taken pity on you, says Yahweh, Your Redeemer." "My love will never leave you, and My covenant of peace with you will never be shaken, says Yahweh who takes pity on you" (Is. 54:8 and 10). His thirst for men's salvation was victory over the thirst inflicted by His executioners.

Death ended the inner struggle of the Savior in upholding His love, pity and pleading while exposed to the flood of evil seeking His removal, the removal of God. Now His task was "accomplished" (Jn. 19:30). Now He could commit His spirit into the Father's hands (Lk. 23:46).

Ours is to be the "mind of Christ" described by St. Paul as the readiness to empty oneself even to suffering the most humiliating death (Phil. 2:6-8), to be "persecuted in the cause of right" (Mt. 5:10). We are followers, members, extensions, messengers of Him Who "suffered outside the gate" and this for the one purpose, "to sanctify the people with His own blood" (Heb. 13:12). And we are called to "go to Him . . . and share His degradation" (Heb. 13:13). This "mind of Christ" is revealed in those words spoken during the extreme ordeal on the cross. They give us a glimpse of that redeeming love in His Heart going out to all men He drew to Himself on the cross (Jn. 12:32).

As we allow Our Lord to transform us into His likeness, so that through us the way would be prepared for His coming into the hearts of men (Mt. 3:3), we come to discover that refusal to love, refusal to work for reconciliation, is to contradict God. We simply refuse the call to be "ambassadors for Christ" (2 Cor. 5:20). "It was God Who reconciled us to Himself through Christ and gave us the work of handing on this reconciliation" (2 Cor 5:18). It is the widespread failure of Christians even to realize their task of bringing about, in their own sphere of life, the unity for which Christ prayed (Jn. 17:21-23) and died.

It is into this world that the Light of the World came (Jn. 8:12), to turn us, His members, into lights of the world by illumination (Mt. 5:14; Eph. 5:14). To close ourselves to the light is to choose eternal death, damnation. "Talk and behave like people who are going to be judged by the law of freedom, because there will be judgment without mercy for those who have not been merciful themselves; but the merciful need have no fear of judgment" (Jas. 2:12-13).

Adultery Committed in the Heart

You have learned how it was said: You must not commit adultery.
But I say this to you: If a man looks at a woman lustfully,
he has already committed adultery in his heart. (5:27-28)

Too often when considering Christian morality or Christian existence, it is not realized that problems—both as to our goals and our failings—must be seen "beyond partial perspectives . . . in the light of an integral vision of man and his vocation, not only his natural and earthly, but also his supernatural and eternal vocation" (Pope Paul VI, *Humanae Vitae*, 7). Our "supernatural and eternal vocation" is revealed reality, entrusted to the *Teaching Church*, the "Oracle of God." We are enabled to live in accord with our divine vocation as we seek and find strength and life from the *Church Sanctifying*, her sacraments and prayers, while her expiations prepare the way for the healing power of God, entrusted to Our Lord Jesus Christ (Mt. 28:18), as He continues to draw all men to Himself (Jn. 12:32). We find our way through the hostile jungle of confusion and deception as we entrust ourselves unconditionally, in faith and hope, to the *Ruling Church*. By her authoritative teaching, her Magisterium (such as Vatican II or the encyclical *Humanae Vitae*) and its living commentaries, the lives of saintly people, we are drawn to a life of purity, of consecration, of holiness.

How thin, even pathetic sound the arguments against the Church, from within and without, in matters of spousal love, marriage, sexuality or procreation if carried on apart from the total vision of man and his destiny. While the social sciences, if pursued with full awareness of their limitations, can expand our knowledge of man, they become misleading or destructive if taken as ultimate truths. Universally accepted criteria used for the description of man, involving a value judgment, such as goodness, wisdom, pride, humility, courage, vanity, generosity, mercy, patience, jealousy, or gentleness, seem to point to the mysterious depth of man, to his heart where good and evil (Mt. 15:19) dwell. It is in terms of such realities and their relation to our position before God that in Shakespeare or Dostoewski, Claudel or Bernanos, we find a depth which is not found in the writings of psychologists or sociologists as they confine themselves to the description of symptoms. Great music is not constructed by means of data supplied by computers, nor did Abraham Lincoln lead the North through the Civil War through opinion polls and preoccupation with his own image and popularity. We abdicate truth if we cease to be judgmental; that is, if we suspect or abandon moral judgments. We thereby become practical atheists, or in relapsing into practical atheism we lose sight of morality. "Once God is forgotten, the creature is lost sight of as well" (*Pastoral Constitution*, 36). "It is only in the Mystery of the Word made flesh that the mystery of man truly becomes clear" (*Pastoral Constitution*, 22).

What is this "Mystery of Man", what are the mysteries that reveal to us "Man", his origin, his destiny, the sources of the contradictions in his being, his potential for good and evil? In broad outlines: man is created, willed by God to share His life, heir to Original Sin, redeemed, and, in this life, called to be "ambassador for Christ" (2 Cor. 5:20). As members of Christ, baptized into Him (Gal. 3:27; Mt. 28:19), and thereby as "Church" we share in the sacramental function of the Church, to be "sign and instrument" (*Dogmatic Constitution*, 1) of Christ, becoming "fellow workers with God" (1 Cor. 3:9). Our journey to eternal life has, through sin, become a Way of the Cross. "Anyone who does not take his cross and follow in My footsteps is not worthy of Me" (Mt. 10:30). "God's foolishness", the Crucifixion of the Son of God, "is wiser than human wisdom" (1 Cor. 1:25). The kingdom of God demands poverty of spirit (Mt. 5:3) and readiness to suffer persecution "in the cause of right" (Mt. 5:10). To live "with the life of Christ" we must be—and remain—crucified with Him (Gal. 2:20,19). "You cannot belong to Christ Jesus unless you crucify all self-indulgent passions and desires" (Gal. 5:24). This is the heart of loving *where* and *as* Christ loves, in fulfillment of the New Commandment (Jn. 13:34), loving even those we find difficult to accept. Yes, love of enemy is commanded (Mt. 5:44, 48). It is obedience without which we would be in opposition to God Whose love for those who turn away from Him and even against Him is the core of redemption (Rom. 5:8)—for "we may be unfaithful, but He is always faithful, for He cannot disown His own self" (2 Tm. 2:13). Redeeming love is of God's essence and made it possible for Him to venture upon man's creation. This love overflows into the Heart of Jesus Who had come (and continues to come in word and sacrament, in the Church, in the brother) "to seek out and save what was lost" (Lk. 19:10).

There is no Christian life, no Christian love among fallen man that does not presuppose, in spite of our reluctance, the wisdom of the Cross. Anything less is deception and fantasy. Love, life, marriage without the cross is cultivating selfishness, a cult of self-indulgence, the hedonism that is anchored into our culture by enormous vested financial interests. Hedonism threatens to *be* our culture. But its fruits are "fornication, gross indecency and sexual irresponsibility; idolatry . . . feuds . . . jealousy . . . envy . . . orgies" (Gal. 5:19-21). And this seems more and more a description of the "free" Western world.

"From the heart come evil intentions: murder, adultery, fornication" (Mt. 15:19). The degradation of woman is first accomplished in the heart. It is incompatible with the respect without which there cannot be love. It is degrading for one who is called to be "the temple of the Holy Spirit" (1 Cor. 6:19) to be a mere instrument of lust on the part of one who also is called by God to be "the temple of the Holy Spirit", but conveniently ignores this reality. An eventually unquestioned life of sexual irresponsibility can deaden all capacity for unselfish love and the sense of purity, for the sacredness of spousal love. The contempt for human rights and dignity can become so all-pervasive that it may become equivalent to actual hatred in the heart which St. John declares to be murder (1 Jn. 3:15). And are not lust and hatred closely related? Is not the blending of pornography, sadism and violence a frightening symptom of our decadence? And it is exactly here that betrayal from within the Church is most notorious, as some theologians, who sneer at the moral teachings of the Church, continue to seek to destroy consciences of the young. Our Lord recommended to drown such "in the depths of the sea with a great millstone round [their] neck" (Mt. 18:6). The wrath of God in the Sacred Heart of Jesus! Statistics of child and teenage prostitution reveal the depth of this rot. We can only conjecture the enormous amount of suffering and, if sanctified suffering, of expiation that prevents the nation from charging "down the cliff" and from perishing as the swine possessed by devils (Mt. 8:32). And we see repeated how "the whole town set out to meet Jesus", imploring Him "to leave the neighborhood". How often do we see in our Catholic institutions of learning, religious communities, and parishes Jesus being asked to "leave"—in the name of compassion—in diabolical inversion of love and compassion. He Who once drove the money changers from the temple (Mt. 21:12-13) is now driven from where once His Kingdom has been. They refuse to hear the Church, and thereby the Lord Jesus, and thereby the Father (Mt. 10:40). "In sight of the city he shed tears over it and said, 'If you . . . had only understood . . . the message of peace! But, alas, it is hidden from your eyes!" Destruction of the city will follow, "because you did not recognize your opportunity when God offered it!" (Lk. 19:41-42, 44).

How can we be followers of Jesus Christ, unless we too offer up "prayer and entreaty, aloud and in silent tears" (Heb. 5:7)? Unless we are willing to expiate, let ourselves be wounded, mocked, insulted, becoming "fools for the sake of Christ" (1 Cor. 4:10)? The only thing we can, with St. Paul, boast about "is the cross of Our Lord Jesus Christ, through whom the world is crucified to me, and I to the world" (Gal. 6:14). With Jesus crucified we must suffer abandonment (Mt. 27:46), thirst (Jn. 19:28) and pray, "Father, forgive them; they do not know what they are doing" (Lk. 23:34).

The hour of darkness—mass murder of the unborn, the systematic corruption of consciences by teachers of religion,—"the power of darkness" (Lk. 22:53) may well be upon us. Thus His Passion began. His Passion continues (Jn. 15:18-23). May we be among those to be crucified, and not among His executioners.

Fight Against Sin to the Point of Death (Hb. 12:4)

If your right eye should cause you to sin, tear it out and throw it away;
for it will do you less harm to lose one part of you than to have
your whole body thrown into hell. And if you right hand should cause
you to sin, cut it off and throw it away; for it will do you less harm
to lose one part of you than to have your whole body go to hell. (5:29-30)

The urgency of facing the massive disorders in the sphere of sexuality compels the Christian to seek and maintain order in his own life and to be informed and firm wherever he becomes responsible for others. The scandal of false and deceptive teaching where truth ought to be taught and cultivated in the "free" Western world, the scandal of well-known theologians still holding on to prestigious teaching positions in universities and seminaries, where they are able to poison the wells, continues. And yet, how can we ignore the words of Our Lord we are considering here, speaking of eternal damnation, of hell for those who refuse to use radical means in defense of purity, for those who compromise, not to speak of "blind men leading blind men" (Mt. 15:14).

We have become permissive, deceiving ourselves into believing that indifference is charity, and we "feel good" in not being "judgmental", while really compromising, even abdicating morality, the very distinction between good and evil. The destruction of morality, of justice, of truth, to be replaced by pragmatic, sociological relativism is now bearing fruit in the growth of murder of the unborn by actual killing; and by virtual murder (1 Jn. 3:15), by that form of hatred which is most deadly, the most icy—total indifference, total contempt, reducing men to the level of animals to be manipulated, without dignity, without rights. I am thinking of the desperate fate of the children of divorced parents—one million in this country added every year. I am thinking of the fate of wives and mothers abandoned by their husbands—alimony shirked, the Law used without consideration of the spouse, of the children that are to be discarded. Is this indifference not the logical consequence of sheer Hedonism, when "fun" and isolated sexuality are seen as the principle ways of finding something that would fill the emptiness of a life "immersed in this world, without hope and without God" (Eph. 2:12)? Is this indifference not the ultimate of hatred, and thus of murder in the heart (1 Jn. 3:15)? Do we see here a unity of evil—a life of rationalized adultery becoming quickly the death of charity, a growing incapacity even to speak, to listen, to sympathize, leading to that total isolation which, if present at the moment of death, will become eternal, will be hell? The Son of God commands us to cut out what causes us to sin, and tells us that the refusal to do so will separate us from God, will throw us into a state of spiritual death and deprive us of the gift of charity, of that love of God which "has been poured into our hearts by the Holy Spirit which has been given to us" (Rom. 5:5). And if there is no conversion, our own self-destruction will go on. "Serpents, brood of vipers, how can you escape being condemned to hell" (Mt. 23:33)? Inevitably cut off *by* ourselves from the source of truth and life, from Almighty God, under the deceptive guise of permissiveness, of love without the cross, the description of unredeemed man given by St. Paul may soon become a portrait of myself—being "foolish, disobedient, led astray, slaves to various passions and pleasures, passing our days in malice and envy, hated by men and hating one another" (Ti. 3:3).

St. Paul's description is that of fallen man before encountering Jesus Christ, before the appearance of "the goodness and loving kindness of God our Savior" (Ti. 3:4). But what if the unclean spirit, having left because of Baptism and Christian education, returns, finding the heart "swept and tidied" (Lk. 11:25), free of charity, hope and faith, enlightened by him who suggested to the Lord to change stones into loaves (Mt. 4:3) and offering Him dominion over the world if only He would worship him, the Prince of this world (Mt. 4:9; Jn. 12:31). What if the "light of the world" (Jn. 8:12) will have been replaced by the Prince of this world who "is on his way to crucify" (Jn. 14:30)? What if the devil—whose existence is of the content of the faith—can become our father, Satan, who "was a murderer from the start . . . in whom there is no truth . . . [who] is a liar and the father of lies" (Jn. 8:44)?

When we try to form some idea of the condition of the world—or of this country—we see man-caused suffering of unprecedented magnitude; and we hear the shallow remedies proposed in terms of a change of structures, as if this would reduce pride, envy, ancient hatreds, sexual irresponsibilities, perversions to stimulate a frozen heart (see Gal. 5:19-20; Rom. 1: 18-32), and relieve their victims, who have been ruthlessly ignored, discarded or manipulated. The word of the Lord that "from the *heart* come evil intentions: murder, adultery, fornication, theft, perjury, slander" (Mt. 15:19) is not considered relevant. It belongs simply to an out-dated wisdom, if not an ancient lie invented to exploit the poor by means of religion—man-made vice to be discarded as science advances, as alchemy and astrology have been discarded.

The radical remedies prescribed by the Lord Jesus when we are tempted to sexual irresponsibilities (Gal. 5:19) and the consequent destruction of marriage and the family remain valid for all times. "Heaven and earth will pass away, but my words will not pass away" (Mk. 13:31). We must radically, that is, with regard to the *roots* of realities revealed and to be believed, with regard to the *roots* of morality, for the sake of man's eternal salvation, we must seek and find (Mt. 7:7) *our* faith in the faith of the Church, as expressed by the Church Teaching, Ruling and Sanctifying. We find it in Scripture, in the teachings of the Councils, in the Creeds, in any statement of the Magisterium, and in the Liturgies formed by revealed truths. But above all, we find the truth in the living testimony or witness (martyrion) of the vast army of Saints, canonized or not, and also right in our midst. Only then will we maintain that courage and fortitude without which faith, hope and charity remain mere decorations, as we "keep up the outward appearance of religion but will have rejected the inner power of it" (2 Tm. 3:5). "Do you know that to be a real Christian, that is to say a Saint, one must have a tender heart within a shell of bronze" (Leon Bloy, *Pilgrim of the Absolute*, p. 283)?

Eternal Hell is as real as the hells in the hearts of men, from which flows all the venom turning the world into an assembly of hells, of Gulags, of slums, families turned into centers of boredom alternating with violence, children virtually or actually being discarded, vast educational enterprises fostering error, confusion, illusion, and skills to be used for aimless progress perpetuating injustices because there is no true wisdom to give direction. And "the wisdom of this world is foolishness to God" (1 Cor. 3:19).

What am I to do? How am I to find Him Who is the Way; where do I find Him Who is the Truth, the Life, the Resurrection (Jn. 14:6; 11:25)? The answer comes from God. The struggle, the power of sin have been with us since the Fall, when man began to hide from God (Gn. 3:8). Entrusting ourselves to the Church, we "set our hearts on His kingdom first, and on His righteousness, and all these other things will be given [us] as well" (Mt. 6:33). "If you make my word your home you will indeed be my disciple" (Jn. 8:31). We face the cost of discipleship as revealed by Our Lord in chapter 10 of the the Gospel of St. Matthew, and as described by St. Paul in the first four chapters of the First Letter to the Corinthians. We "will learn the truth and the truth will make [us] free" (Jn. 8:32). The word of God will find in us "rich soil" (Mt. 13:23). We will lead a life of Hope, avoiding the presumption of sitting in judgment on God's word and the despair of rationalizing the evil in our hearts in terms of practical conformity to the pressures of our world that is heading for destruction (Jas. 4:1-3). The Church is our Mother, our Teacher; Christ rules us through her. We will hold on to the warning of St. Paul, to "work out [our] salvation in fear and trembling" (Phil. 2:12). With the obedience of faith, we will look to Him Who is "the light of the world". "Anyone who follows Me will not be walking in the dark; he will have the light of life" (Jn. 8:12), "that light of Christ which shines out visibly from the Church" (*Dogmatic Constitution*, 1). Then we will again become "innocent and genuine, perfect children of God among a deceitful and underhand brood, and [we] will shine in the world like bright stars" (Phil. 2:15).

Expiation—Vocation for the Abandoned Spouse

It has also been said: Anyone who divorces his wife must give her

a writ of dismissal! But I say this to you: Everyone who divorces his wife,
except for the case of fornication, makes her an adulteress;
anyone who marries a divorced woman commits adultery. (5:31:32)

The bond of sacramental marriage is unbreakable. "Authentic married love is caught up in divine love and is directed and enriched by the redemptive power of Christ and the salvific action of the Church" (*Pastoral Constitution*, 48). What follows from this for the abandoned spouse? In such a situation, can the sacrament be more than a barrier to entering a new covenant of marriage? As more and more marriages are broken by one of the spouses, what is the vocation of the abandoned spouse? Is it only resignation, a life of celibacy, imposed by the violence of breaking the marriage bond?

If then infidelity of one spouse has become permanent, it becomes a rejection of the redemptive love of Christ, a repudiation of the life-giving saving bond of Christ and His Church, a recapitulation of the Crucifixion, which, on a cosmic scale, has been the consummation of man's rejection of God, working itself out against God Who had become vulnerable in Jesus. Here the target of rejection is the faithful spouse, and he or she becomes the victim suffering Crucifixion renewed by one person upon another. The most sacred love possible between human beings, "enriched by the redemptive power of Christ and the salvific action of the Church," is being strangled in the heart of the spouse abandoning the other, while the same love is being crucified in the faithful spouse.

How would the "mind of Christ" (Phil. 2:5) we are to acquire be realized in the victim, in the abandoned spouse? To repeat, is resignation to a celibate life the foremost task? Or can there, for a member of Christ, be a deeper aspect of the "mind of Christ" that would for the victim, in faith and hope, be a sharing of that redeeming charity revealed by Christ in His ordeal and death? Could the suffering "make up," in this particular historical situation, something "that has still to be undergone by Christ for the sake of His Body, the Church" (Col. 1:24)? What Christ as victim achieved on the cross, can this become reality at this historical moment? The sufferings of Christ contained the suffering inflicted on the abandoned spouse, to be conquered, in tentative absolution of the guilty one, by His redeeming love for the spouse who had, by his or her sin, become executioner of the abandoned spouse, and thereby co-executioner of Jesus Christ.

As His sufferings were transformed by love from being the intended destruction of the Divine into the very source of power of redemption, could this not be a paradigm for those "who have been crucified with Christ," and now are emptied of self, of self-seeking, so that they may now come, not to live with [their] own life, but with the life of Christ Who lives in [them]" (Gal. 2 19-20)? Now brutal suffering, frustration and resignation can be transformed into redemptive suffering for the sake of the spouse who has deserted spouse and children. It becomes "the cross of Jesus Christ, through which the world," the deserter, "is crucified" to the abandoned spouse, and the abandoned spouse to the world, to the deserter. The cross, meant to tear apart, becomes, through a victory of love, a source of redeemed unity.

The bond continues to exist, though one spouse has sought to break it. The salvation of the spouse deserted remains responsibility of the abandoned spouse. It now becomes his or her task to enter upon a Way of the Cross for the salvation of the unfaithful spouse. To respond to the fearful sufferings of abandonment becomes a recapitulation, on a small scale, of that love maintained in a bitter interior struggle by Our Lord when he suffered the world's rejection.

To suffer for the sake of the deserter can hardly be considered a strict obligation, but it may well be a call from God. It would be, for the abandoned spouse, a share in the vocation of contemplatives, in their expiation on behalf of others. Spiritual advice in such cases is to be given with the greatest delicacy, without any pressure. At a period of time when mysticism is "interesting," this interest should not lead to a gnostic elitism—a great danger for all involved, endangering the very relation with God of the spouse seeking to become a sacrifice for the deserter. As guide in such a delicate concern, we may follow the instructions given by St. Paul to the Philippians preceding the description of the spirit in which these instructions are to be followed, the spirit that ought to form all life to be called Christian, the Mind of Christ that must be recapitulated in us. He "emptied Himself . . . obedient unto death, even death on a cross" (Phil. 2:1-8). Love is to be seen as obedience, irrespective of one's liking or aversions, of one's frequent inclinations to contempt, hatred, revenge—all temptations to sin. The persevering pleading and suffering on behalf of the spouse must remain carefully hidden, and except in confidential conversation with a spiritual guide, is not to be revealed. It would be a disaster if this hidden apostolate came to the attention of the spouse for whom it is meant. The spirit of this apostolate is to be a blending of the Beatitude of mourning and of being persecuted in the cause of right (Mt. 5:5,10). Both Beatitudes are implementations of Poverty of Spirit, which is so well described in Paul's instructions to the Philippians just referred to (2:1-4). For in them is realized on the ordinary level of Christian existence the following of Him Who had emptied Himself even unto "death on a cross."

Christian love of neighbor is to love *where* and *as* God loves. His love is now channeled through the Heart of Jesus, and goes out to those, to us, who have broken His Heart, who were then, and continue to be among those He drew to Himself when He "was lifted up from the earth" (Jn. 12:32). Our longing in faith, that is, in realization of the revealed realities, above all of the redeeming, crucified and glorified love of Jesus Our Lord—a love now clothed with "all authority in heaven and on earth" (Mt. 28:18)—our longing in faith becomes now a redeeming hope, ready to prepare the way for God's redeeming grace. This love of God, this now also human love of the glorified Christ—"the power of His resurrection" (Phil. 3:11)—communicated to us, accepted by us, can now be radiated by us, to become a historical reality here and now, in and through us. This radiating belongs to the order of grace and may remain totally hidden.

In the Providence of God, men are called to prepare the way for God's grace. As we enter into and share the desire of God for the salvation of all (1 Tim. 2:4), we become fellow-workers of God (2 Cor. 6:1). We become "ambassadors for Christ." "It is as though God were appealing through us" (2 Cor. 5:20). As Christ's members, as "Church," we share in the sacramentality of the Church, as revelation and instrument of Him of Whom the Church, in turn, is revelation and instrument, Jesus Christ, Who is now Our Lord. In prayer and expiation we become willing to bear the crosses, the burdens rejected by those for whom we pray and are ready to suffer the consequences of their failures, of their rejected burdens. This is the Law of Christ (Gal. 6:2).

Would it be asking too much of those who render the care and love of the Good Shepherd present in the Church—and this might become a responsibility shared by diocesan marriage tribunals—to suggest to the abandoned spouses the apostolate of expiation on behalf of the spouse who has broken the marriage? Could the abandoned spouse be led to see in this cross and deprivation an apostolate, even if it would have to remain hidden from the world, and even if visible success can rarely be hoped for?

In this context celibacy too can, for an abandoned spouse, become part of a powerful apostolate that will prepare the way not only for the one who has placed a heavy cross on his or her spouse and children. It will, invisibly, become a light and a source of grace for many. To the victim the words of St. Paul can now be applied with a new and deeper significance: "I have been crucified with Christ, and I live now not with my own life but with the life of Christ Who lives in me" (Gal. 2:19-20). And the victim will become an apostle with a deeper realization of the words of Paul, "You have died, and now the life you have is hidden with

Christ in God." And the promise: "but when Christ is revealed—and
He is your life—you too will be revealed in all your glory with Him"
(Col. 3:3-4).

To Follow Him Who is the Truth

Again you have learnt how it was said to our ancestors:
you must not break your oath, but must fulfill your oaths to the Lord.
But I say to you: do not swear at all, either by heaven,
since that is God's throne; or by the earth, since that is his footstool;
or by Jerusalem, since it is the city of the great king. Do not swear
by your own head either, since you cannot turn a single hair either white
or black. All you need to say is "Yes" if you mean yes, or "No" if you
mean no; anything more than this comes from the evil one. (5:33-37)

"You must speak the truth to one another, since we are all members of one another" (Eph. 4:25). "If we live by the truth and in love, we
shall grow in all ways *into* Christ, who is the head." (Eph. 4:15).

Goodness and holiness are inseparable from truth, from the realities revealed by God, of Himself, of "the great works of God" (Acts
2:11), of man, of the hazards and the goal of man's life—in short, of
God revealing Himself as Creator and Savior, "Being and Love . . . ineffably the *same* divine Reality of Him Who has wished to make Himself
known to us" (Credo). To these truths we say "Yes". We are to say
"No" to what contradicts them, distorts them, diminishes them, in short,
to all errors and lies about them. And here we may well remember that
lies can be meant for others, but also for myself. The latter is called
"rationalizing" and is the foundation of sin intended and committed.
For sin is a lived lie.

Would it be reading too much into the words of Our Lord—to
simply say "Yes" if we mean yes, and "No" if we mean no—to apply it
to the origins and intentions of lying in our lives? Lying to others, lying
to myself? And that anything obscuring what we ought to say, that anything meant to mislead, to cover up, to falsify by false emphasis, "comes
from the evil one"? That we are to remember "that man who infringes
even one of the least of these commandments *and* teaches to others to
do the same" lies to himself ("infringes") and to others ("teaches others"), and that this is how man, mankind, political, economic life become and remain alienated from truth, become destructive of the kingdom of God, of the kingdom of Him who was, and remains, "a sign that
is spoken against" (Lk. 2:34).

"You must speak the truth to one another, since we are all members of one another" (Eph. 4:25) under Christ the head in redeemed unity, as we are being drawn to and into Him (Jn. 12:32). This unity of faith (Eph. 4:5) requires an unconditional "Yes" to the Trinity and the Incarnation because it is the Faith of the Church, which in turn is "the oracle of God". "When a man has become a Catholic, were he to set about following out a doubt which has occurred to him, *he has already disbelieved* . . . He fell from grace at the moment when he deliberately entertained and pursued this doubt" (Newman, *Faith and Doubt*, p 218). The words will sound to some outrageous, arrogant, narrow, outright stupid and could not possibly express all that is implicit in the Faith of Catholics from Peter to Pope John Paul II and till the end of history. They will tell us that it is uncharitable to declare dissenters as no longer belonging to the Catholic Church. That the willingness to dialogue about the teachings of the Magisterium is sign of an open mind, a sort of self-declared charity. Do not majorities determine and, if necessary, re-interpret truths about God and His ways and expectations into something more acceptable for modern man? But then, to say "Yes" when we *mean* yes, and "No" when we *mean* no, would presuppose that we *mean* something. And that might cost us popularity and jobs. Often it is academic suicide, as many can verify.

"There is One Body, one Spirit, just as you were called *into* one and the same hope when you were called. There is one Lord, one faith, one baptism, and one God who is Father *of all, over all, through all* and *within all*" (Eph. 4:4-6).

These are realities revealed, descriptive of the Mystery of the Church, the God-given extension of Christ, the Sacrament of Christ, as His communicated presence, revelation and instrument. To share in this continuing function of Christ in the Church is the task, the vocation of every Christian. "The Christian vocation is, of its nature, a vocation to the apostolate as well". "From the fact of their union with Christ the head flows the layman's right and duty to be apostles. Inserted as they are in the Mystical Body of Christ by Baptism and strengthened by the power of the Holy Spirit in Confirmation, it is by the Lord himself that they are assigned to the apostolate" (*Decree on the Apostolate of Lay People*, 2 and 3). This vocation, this God-given responsibility for the salvation, for the bringing "everything together under Christ, as head" (Eph. 1:10), is the guiding, because the highest, dimension of human existence. It is to be given, in itself and in the duties derived from it, our unconditional "Yes", while every distortion or infringement is to be given our unconditional "No".

There can be no exception to God being the Father *of* all, in His providence *over* all, in His engaging us in the Apostolate *through* all, and our becoming one in Him as He, the Father, in the Son and the Son, with the Father and the Holy Spirit, live in us. Coming "to share the divine nature" (2 Peter 1:4), the Father becomes Father *within* us. This is the goal of creation. Because "when everything is subjected to Him, then the Son himself will be subject in his turn to the One who subjected all things to Him, so that God [the Father] may be all in all" (2 Cor. 15:28). "At that time, together with the human race, the universe itself, which is so closely related to man and *which attains its destiny through him*"—a remarkable statement of vast implications— "will be perfectly reestablished in Christ (cf. Eph. 1:10; Col. 1:20; 2 Peter 3:10-13)" (*Dogmatic Constitution*, 48).

Unconditional "Yes" to truths revealed, to their revealed interrelations and mutual illumination, is to live by realities that are revealed because they belong to God "whose home is in inaccessible light" (1 Tim. 6:16). We believe that they are from God, that they are entrusted to the Church, that they are constitutive of the Church teaching, ruling and sanctifying. A "No" to any truth is a "No" to God. It is exclusion from God Whom, by our "No" we have first excluded from our very being. In evil, in self-destruction, in progress on the road to damnation, the initiative is ours, as in love and union with God the initiative belongs to God, Who has "loved us first" (1 John 4:19).

"It was to undo all that the devil has done that the Son of God appeared" (1 John 3:8). Of this undoing we are to be both object and instrument. In our conflict with "The Sovereignties and the Powers who originate the darkness in this world, the spiritual army of evil in the heavens" (Eph. 6:12), compromise, hesitancy, the smallest dishonesties are betrayal, for we are dealing with mighty, pure Intelligences, fallen Angels. In this combat there can be no "Yes, yes, and No, no, at the same time" (2 Cor. 1:17). That is why "anything more" than "Yes" or No", any rationalizing about what God means or demands, is not imperfection but the beginning of lying to ourselves. Abortion cannot be called "Free Choice". Abortion cannot "almost always" be wrong. And to mislead thus with the added lies of pretending that it is an option open to the followers of Jesus Christ by teaching it as a Catholic theologian is simply to get more deeply entangled in lies. And sin is lived lie. To teach that Christ did not know that He would rise again (Mt. 16:21) is to relegate His clear words in the Gospels to deceptions added later. One such lie about the words of Christ destroys the veracity of the word of God. The collapse that follows is all around us.

"Yes", if we mean yes, "No", if we mean no—there is no "yes and no", there is no relativism when God's truths are at stake.

Truth is the name of God, is sacred. Taking truth lightly, twisting it to our convenience is the beginning of spiritual sickness tending, if not stopped by the voice of appointed shepherds, to death of the Church in the hearts of men. With the destruction of truth, the ultimate truth, of true metaphysics and the truths of revelation of which the shepherds are the guardians, justice and charity too will disappear from the world once truth has been dethroned.

In our culture we are surrounded by many cynical manipulations designed for commercial and political purposes. To manipulate, a deadening of the intelligence is needed. This can be done in many ways. Silliness, escapes into fantasy, flattering clichés, flight from reality in preparation for and in support of flight from God. The Mass is often misunderstood and "staged" as a device to bring people together and make them "feel good", so they can be deceived, leading them to some emotional reaction taken as religious experience; thus they are weaned from the mysterious, ineffable reality of the Sacred Act. The sacred texts are often translated so badly that celebrants and participants are deprived of what ought to be the prayers of the Church.

Renewal of the Church, the cleansing of the temple of God, depends intrinsically and essentially on truth, on the ability to know in faith, to *want* to know in hope, to "speak the truth in love" (Eph. 4:15). It is the God-given restoration of the ability to "say 'Yes' if you mean yes, 'No' if you mean no" (Mt. 5:37). It is the restoration of genuine culture as expressed in language, in wisdom, in links with the past, sound vision of the future, and a sane response to nature. Otherwise, there will be no analogies from the created world by means of which the supernatural can be reached and expressed. The lack of access to natural analogies to point to the supernatural stifles the growth of religious knowledge, the building up of the content of the faith in men's hearts and minds. All this we witness today on an ever increasing scale. Appearance over content—the white-washed sepulchers, whose content are "dead men's bones and every kind of corruption" (Mt. 23:27).

And so we pray, "Thy kingdom come"—a "kingdom of *truth* and life, a kingdom of holiness and grace, a kingdom of justice, love and peace" (Preface for the Feast of Christ the King).

Reckless Generosity

*You have learnt how it was said: Eye for eye and tooth for tooth.
But I say to you: offer the wicked man no resistance. On the contrary,
if anyone hits you on the right cheek, offer him the other as well;*

if a man takes you to law and would have your tunic,
let him have your cloak as well, and if anyone orders you
to go one mile, go two miles with him. Give to anyone who asks,
and if anyone wants to borrow, do not turn away. (5:38-42)

The words of Our Lord we are trying to consider speak of reckless, unconditional generosity, free of any intention to shame or to demonstrate. They speak of spontaneous trust in faith and hope, in response to the divine will when we are confronted with wickedness. Human ideas, human action, human words, though necessarily limited, are here used to stretch out to infinite reality, to break through to the Triune God of infinite power and knowledge, wisdom and holiness. Here we will have the infinity, the total incomprehensibility of the reality of God "whose home is in inaccessible light" (1 Tm. 6:16), and man in unconditional hope flinging himself into God's design, into the ways of divine Providence.

God, loving (1 Jn. 4:19) and seeking (Rev. 3:19) us *first*, enables us to learn of His merciful love by His gift of faith. The divine gift of hope allows us to transcend our paralyzing sin to long for deliverance. By God's gift of charity, "poured into our hearts by the Holy Spirit" (Rm. 5:5), once we "share the divine nature" (2 Pt. 1:4) and have made our home in Jesus, the true vine (Jn. 15:4)—in charity, our union with life and love with God comes to life. God seeks man, while enabling man to seek Him. God's seeking is now carried out by the human heart of Jesus; man's seeking God demands the leap of faith and the recklessness of hope.

God's motives and methods are "impossible to penetrate . . . or understand." It is the God of Whom St. Paul wrote that "all that exists comes from him; all is by him and for him" (Rm. 11:33,36). The words of Our Lord we are considering describe the recklessness of the saints, of a Maximilian Kolbe, a Francis Xavier, of the widow putting "everything she possessed, all she had to live on" into the temple treasury (Mk. 12:44), but above all the recklessness of her who accepted God's call to be the Mother of the redeemer, of Whom she knew from the prophesies that He was to become "more worm than man" (Ps. 22:6), "a thing despised and rejected by men", Who would bear all our sufferings and sorrows (Is. 53:2-3).

The Christian vocation, Christian life, Christian commandments are unfathomable, limitless in their goal, in their reach, in their scope because they open up into the infinity of the Godhead. Are we not created and called "to share in the divinity of Christ (2 Pt 1:4), who humbled Himself to share in our humanity" (Mass, Preparation of the Wine)? The eternal Son, "true God from true God", emptied Himself by assuming human nature, entering human history in order to wrest men from eternal perdition. And yet, when we consider history in Christian times lived by Christians, is there a change of direction? Was the prayer of Jesus heard that we may "all be one" as the Son lives in the Father and the Father in the Son (Jn. 17:21) in a unity rooted in Love (the Holy Spirit)? And is the Trinity—the source and pattern of unity among men—reflected and revealed among men, who thereby give witness to the divine origin of unity?

Christian behavior on the visible, historical level, seems at times to create almost an iron curtain between God Whose name is "Love" (1 Jn. 4:8,16), Who lived among us (Jn. 1:14) and promised to be with us always, to the end of time (Mt. 28:20), and the Christian world. How is it reasonably possible for Christians to remain faithful, and for others, to discover the Church of Jesus Christ?

But His "is not a kingdom of this world" (Jn. 18:36). "The coming of the kingdom of God does not admit of observation and there will be no one to say 'Look here! Look there!' For you must know, the kingdom of God is among you" (Lk. 17:20-21). The life of the Christian is "hidden with Christ in God" (Col. 3:3). The pattern of the history of Christianity, contained, though often overgrown and hidden, within Christendom; and even more deeply hidden in post-Christian, present history—the pattern is that of the life of Jesus on earth, and of the first, most perfect manifestation of the Church on earth, Mary. God comes and calls in silence, preparing man's heart. But a moment comes, when man must do violence to himself (Mt. 11:12) to leap from limitation to the freedom of God's children. "You must put aside your old self, which gets corrupted by following illusory desires. Your mind must be renewed by a spiritual revolution so that you can put on the new self that has been created in God's way, in the goodness and holiness of the truth" (Eph. 4:22-24).

The recklessness of the saints described by Our Lord in the words we are considering, the initial recklessness of first or second conversion, must again be renewed. It is to become a habitual recklessness, otherwise ours is not a life of faith, hope and charity. The initial temptation, to usurp the place of God (Gn. 3:5) lives on in all of us, reinforced by "the devil's tactics". "We have to struggle . . . against . . . the spiritual army of evil . . . [which] originates the darkness in this world" (Eph. 6:11-12). But "this is the victory over the world—our faith" (1 Jn. 5:4).

If the words of Our Lord seem to us exaggerated, impractical, meant for extraordinary saints, we are deceiving ourselves. Suffice it here calmly to examine some other words of His. "Anyone who does not take his cross and follow in my footsteps"—from the Praetorium to

Calvary—"is not worthy of me. Anyone who finds his life will lose it; anyone who loses his life for my sake will find it" (Mt. 10:38-39). There is no middle way: "since you are neither cold nor hot . . . but only luke-warm, I will spit you out of my mouth" (Rv. 3:15-16). Does not the Church suffer from the refusal of so many to remain faithful to God's call, in marriage, priesthood, religious life, and as Shepherds, as Bish-ops? Is not fidelity to the end a condition for salvation? The only alter-native is final impenitence. Without the recklessness described by Our Lord we will simply prefer sin to suffering and death. Only "the man who stands firm until the end will be saved" (Mt. 24:13). Does not the "mind of Christ" revealed in the emptying Himself of the eternal Son into human existence, service and death, even death on a cross, in obe-dience to the Father, reveal the Father's will? And is not this to be *our* mind, our disposition (Phil. 2:5-8)?

Though "in fear and trembling", and realizing that it is God "who puts both the will and the action into us" (Phil. 2:13), we simply cannot be followers of Jesus Christ, we cannot be "on the way to salvation" (1 Cor. 1:18) without the Cross. "None of you can be my disciple unless he gives up all his possessions" (Lk. 14:33). The language of Jesus is radi-cal, goes to the root, because He had to redeem us from eternal damna-tion and enable us to seek and find, through and in him, eternal life. On our part this requires frequent radical breaks with temptation and sin. And this calls for the radical recklessness in faith and hope which Our Lord described. His words show us what it is to pray unconditionally, "Thy will be done." Nothing could be more reckless.

Love of Enemies

*You have learned how it was said: You must love your neighbor
and hate your enemy. But I say this to you: love your enemies
and pray for those who persecute you; in this way you will be sons
of your Father in heaven, for he causes His sun to rise on bad men
as well as good, and His rain to fall on honest and dishonest men alike.
For if you love those who love you, what right have you to claim
any credit? Even the tax collectors do as much, do they not? And if
you save your greetings for your brothers are you doing anything
exceptional? Even the pagans do as much, do they not? You must
therefore be perfect just as your heavenly Father is perfect. (5:43-48)*

The true living God, Who revealed Himself to Israel, and to the world in Jesus Christ, Whom to see is to see the Father (Jn. 14:9), "whose home is in inaccessible light" (1 Tm. 6:16), is not an impersonal creative power, completely inescapable and completely "other." "He is He Who Is, as revealed to Moses (Ex. 3:14); and He is Love (1 Jn. 4:8, 16), as the Apostle John teaches us: so that these two names, Being and Love, express ineffably the same divine Reality of Him Who has wished to make Himself known to us" (Credo of Pope Paul VI). This is the Good News, the Gospel, that the Creator is not a crushing power, but that He is Love, crucifiable Love, vulnerable, as we learn from the tears shed by Jesus Christ lamenting the blindness of His people, of His City Jerusalem.

In Him, in the Lord Jesus Christ, are often seen facets of the Love which God *is*—tears shed on the hill above Jerusalem, tears at His friend Lazarus' tomb, silent tears in long nights of "prayer and entreaty" (Heb. 5:7), tears on the Cross, when the weight of the World's Sin crushed Him, "now more worm than man" (Ps. 22:6), "a thing despised and rejected by men" (Is. 53:3). Facets of this Love—"being patient with [us] all, wanting nobody to be lost and everybody to be brought to change his ways" (2 Pt. 3:9). "I am gentle and humble in heart" (Mt. 11:29) said the Lord Jesus, Whom to see [and hear] is to see [and to hear] the Father (Jn. 14:9). "How often have I longed to gather your children, as a hen gathers her brood under her wings, and you refused" (Lk. 13:34): this reveals another facet of the God Who *is* Love. The mystery of our Redemption is contained in the word of total redeeming love spoken while suffering total rejection: "Father, forgive them; they do not know what they are doing" (Lk. 24:34). The Church, in her Scripture, her Sacraments, her prayers and expiations, extends God, Love, into a world which in accepting Him, extends Him, and in rejecting or ignoring Him, continues to crucify Him in her members (Col. 1:24), who in turn are called to absorb evil in good, to "resist evil and conquer it with good" by that victory of Love achieved on Calvary which is now to be rendered historically present through His members.

The very real contradiction between a Creator of infinite power and knowledge and creating wisdom, and a world in which Cardinal Newman could see no reflection of its Creator has been bridged by the very same, only one God when He became Man, accepting the inevitable consequences of drawing to Himself all rejections throughout history. Here God, in His assumed humanity, could be the target and victim of all sin to conquer it with love, the *love of enemy*. And thus the God Creator is no longer "The Other", incompatible with created freedom, but the God of Creative Love, "meek and humble in heart", the God who loved us first (1 Jn. 4:19), Who "is always faithful" though we be unfaithful, "for he cannot disown his own self" (2 Tm. 2:13), the divine Self, Whose name is Love. "His love endures for ever" (Ps. 136).

"With everlasting love I have taken pity on you, says Yahweh, your redeemer" (Is. 54:8). "And when I am lifted up from the earth, I shall draw all men to myself" (Jn. 12:32).

Have we now begun to grasp that the "two names" [of God], Being and Love not only "express ineffably the *same* divine Reality of Him Who has wished to make Himself known to us" (*Credo*, Pope Paul VI), but that they are, for our redemption, at each other's service? As God extends His redeeming love to us, he has His infinite creative power at the service of His love. Inaccessible mystery! All redeeming love of God for men is love of those who see in God their enemy: "What proves that God loves us is that Christ died for us while we were still sinners" (Rom. 5:8). But before we can say Christ died *for* us, we must remember that He died *through* us. "Yahweh burdened him with the sins of all of us" (Is. 53:6). All sin is against God—"Having sinned against none other than you" (Ps. 51:4). "Father, I have sinned against heaven and against you", said the Prodigal (Lk. 15:21). Both actual sins, and the dispositions from which they spring and which sin forms and strengthens, both imply the wish that God would step aside, would ignore the lie I live in sinning, the lie I rationalize by putting my intelligence, my capacity for truth, in the service of self and in opposition to the source and, as Creator, the author of all truth. For the Christian, grave sin implies a suspension of faith and of hope, through presumption and despair, often alternating; and of charity, turning to a life of self-indulgence (Gal. 5:19-21).

We have set ourselves on the road toward enmity with God, to grow into His enemies, destructive of our true selves, of our capacity and fitness for God. Thus we are blocking divine Providence for which we are "to prepare a way . . . make straight his paths", to be a voice giving witness in the wilderness, in a world that is largely God-less (Jn. 15:18-19; Phil. 2:15). And yet, there remains the fidelity of God's love for me (2 Tm. 2:13), of God the Redeemer, a love that is extended to me by the Good Shepherd (Jn. 10:14-18). As we repent, in conversion, we come to know that even our betrayals do not make of God an enemy, that even men and mankind have not been able to discourage and undermine His love.

"Yahweh looked with favor on Abel" and his offering. The beauty of Abel's God-given holiness made Cain "angry and downcast", and Cain killed his brother. Thus began the long chain of hatreds that is human history. Hatred of God's image and likeness, of purity of heart that is required to know and to see God (Mt. 5:8), of innocence, of compassion, mercy, and that longing and ability to give, to empty oneself in poverty of spirit: for the "ill disposed, is not sin at the door like a crouching beast hungering for you" (Gn. 4:4-8)? Hatred, the blinding, inexorable will to destroy the beautiful, the true, the noble, holiness—trace, revelation, presence of God,—how can those in whom this will to destruction is at work be loved?

Voice of the Eternal Father: "I did forsake you for a brief moment, but with great love I will take you back. In excess of anger, for a moment I hid my face from you. But with everlasting love I have taken pity on you, says Yahweh, your redeemer" (Is. 54:7-8). The infinite Creator of the universe pleading with His people! "The mountains may depart, the hills may be shaken, but my love for you will never leave you" (Is. 54:10). "Let the wicked man abandon his way, the evil man his thoughts. Let him turn back to Yahweh who will take pity on him, to our God who is rich in forgiving; for my thoughts are not your thoughts, my ways not your ways" (Is. 55:7-8). "Yahweh is tender and compassionate, slow to anger, most loving, his indignation does not last for ever, his resentment exists a short time only; he never treats us, never punishes us, as our guilt and our sins deserve" (Ps. 103:8-10).

Prayers of the Incarnate Son, Jesus Christ, Son of Mary: "Father, forgive them; they do not know what they are doing" (Lk. 23:34). And in the Garden, "and going a little further he fell on his face and prayed. 'My Father,' he said, 'if it is possible, let this cup pass me by. Nevertheless, let it be as you, not I, would have it' " (Mt. 26:39). "Let us go! My betrayer is already close at hand" (Mt. 29: 46). "During His life on earth, He offered up prayer and entreaty, aloud and in silent tears" (Heb. 5:7). And now, "He is living for ever to intercede for all who come to God through Him" (Heb. 7:25). "There, at God's right hand He stands and pleads for us" (Rom. 8:34). Yes, "if anyone should sin, we have our advocate with the Father, Jesus Christ, who is just; He is the sacrifice that takes our sins away, and not only ours, but the whole world's" (1 Jn. 2:1-2).

The Voice, the Prayer of man: Abraham, pleading with God for Sodom (Gn. 18:16-32), Moses pleading for his people (Ex. 32:11-14), as both continue now in heaven. And the prayer of St. Stephen, the first Christian martyr, "Lord, do not hold this sin against them" (Acts 7:60). And the millions of voices constantly rising to God, asking for mercy for others, for all—the Church Praying—and wherever such prayers are offered, where such hope for others and for all is alive, there the Church is mysteriously present (*Dogmatic Constitution*, 16). It is always obedience to the New Commandment, to love *where* God loves, *as* God loves, a love now filling the Sacred Heart of Jesus, the Heart we broke but which remained faithful, for God, dwelling in the Heart of Jesus, "cannot disown his own self" (2 Tm. 2:13). And His name *is* Love (1 Jn. 4:8,16).

The redeeming love of Jesus Christ has its origins in the Father. "As the Father has loved me, so I have loved you" (Jn. 15:9)—communication of Love. In Jesus the extension of the Father's love to men is an obedience (". . . as I have kept my Father's commandment") to love by being "obedient unto death, even death on a cross" (Phil. 2:8), and in the same obedience to remain faithful in his love for men, drawing "all men to [himself]" (Jn. 12:32). And for the further extension of this love into the world *we* are now commanded: "love your enemies and pray for those who persecute you; in this way [we] will be sons of [our] Father . . . and be perfect just as [our] heavenly Father is perfect" (Mt. 5:44-45, 48).

"Try, then, to imitate God, as children of his that he loves, and follow Christ by loving as he loved you, giving himself up in our place as a fragrant offering and a sacrifice to God." (Eph. 5:1-2).

IV

Humility

Almsgiving in Secret

Be careful not to parade your good deeds before men to attract
their notice; by doing this you will lose all reward from your Father
in heaven. So when you give alms, do not have it trumpeted before you;
this is what the hypocrites do in the synagogues and in the streets to win
men's admiration. I tell you solemnly, they have their reward.
But when you give alms, your left hand must not know
what your right hand is doing; your almsgiving must be secret,
and your Father who sees all that is done in secret will reward you.(6:1-4)

"God does not see as man sees; man looks at appearances but Yahweh looks at the heart" (1 Sm. 16:7). This country would undergo a profound crisis if the word of Our Lord were taken to heart by our leading citizens, by politicians, by the judiciary, by leaders in industry and commerce, by artists, not to speak of scholars. The word of Christ speaks of objectivity, of disinterested-ness—a new orientation that, in our present culture, would seem almost unthinkable. Success, approval, popularity, influence, power rather than self-effacing living seem to be the ideal almost universally proclaimed, putting the vast number of humble people at a great disadvantage. Discarding much of our common motivations, we must consider again the common good, justice, and live by the ancient principle that to suffer injustice is *better* (for the Christian: imperative, a sacred obligation, essential to being a follower of Christ, necessary for salvation) than to commit injustice. We must restrain personal ambition and vanity: give up the illusion that wealth is the door to freedom; follow Him Who had not come "to be served but to serve" (Mt. 20:28): see greed as idolatry (Col. 3:5): refuse the degradation of sexuality in advertisement, entertainment and life style: be known for rejection of certain practices accepted by society, in politics and sports; be ready to live by the wisdom of God which to men is foolishness (1 Cor. 1:17-31), ready to live by the eighth beatitude (a necessary condition for the Kingdom of God), be prepared to suffer persecution in the cause of right (Mt. 5:10) rather than betraying God's trust—in short, to test all decisions before God Who sees the heart, before Whom no life can stand.

Such is the conversion demanded by Our Lord, the putting aside of the "old self, which gets corrupted by following illusory desires . . . [to] be renewed by a spiritual revolution . . . [to] put on the new self that has been created in God's own way, in the goodness and holiness of the

83

truth" (Eph. 4:22-24). It is all contained in the new Commandment—*commandment*, not suggestion,—to love one another just as the Lord Jesus loved us, and continues to love us (Jn. 13:34).

The word of Our Lord we are considering speaks of alms. But all free activities of man must be in the service of men as our brothers and sisters in Christ, must have the character of "alms", all men must be loved as Christ loves (Jn. 13:34) Who gave "his life as a ransom for many" (Mt. 20:38). All of human existence is entrusted to us by God (Gn. 1:28), flowing from God's self-giving; it should be motivated by the will to serve whatever the cost, in a spirit of self-effacing disinterestedness. Our existence must be modeled after the central intention of the Lord Jesus, Who "did not cling to his equality with God, but emptied himself" (Phil. 2:6-7). The "emptying Himself" began with the Incarnation of the eternal Son, "true God from true God", and came to perfection in obedience of "death on a cross" (Phil. 2:8) while, in obedience, enveloping His destroyers in unspeakable love, a love loved with the perfection of all parental and brotherly love. It is a love totally emptied of any self-seeking, absolutely objective, never reflecting on the advantage of the lover. It was, in Jesus Christ, at every moment of His life on earth, an incarnation, that is, an assumption of human life and activity, of human intention in spirit and content, in disposition and task. And it was an incarnation ultimately by the eternal Son, Who eternally is subsistent, personified Altruism, total self-giving, total relation, eternally begotten of the Father, eternally Gift received and Gift given. The human life of Jesus was a total gift from the beginning—"God, here I am! I am coming to obey your will" (Heb. 10:7)—to the bitter end—"Father, into your hands I commit my spirit" (Lk. 23:46). "Christ did not please himself" (Rom. 15:3). His human beginning, His life and death were an extension into a rebellious, self-seeking, brutal, proud and envious world, of the Son of God, perfect, pure and generous in His love. And we are to be, and become even more perfectly, His members, His further extension, His co-workers (1 Cor. 3:9), "part of God's household" (Eph. 2:19), "in him ... being built into a house where God lives in the spirit" (Eph. 2:22). Nothing less.

What Our Lord teaches here as necessary for almsgiving to be pleasing to God applies to any giving on our part, which is always a giving of self, a service done to those whom God loves and therefore *to* God, but also, *for, on behalf* of God, as His fellow workers (1 Cor. 3:9), as "ambassadors for Christ" (2 Cor. 5:20).

To learn and practice unreflecting generosity in the service of God and of men, in obedience to the two great commandments that contain "the whole law and the Prophets" (Mt. 22:40), is our great spiritual task today. It is more difficult today, because the reflective spirit is a powerful and paralyzing force. It is increasingly important because, in the Western world, Christian existence will assume increasingly the character of "a sign that is rejected" (Lk. 2:34), "to the pagans madness" (1 Cor. 1:23). The wisdom of God makes us "fools for the sake of Christ", to be "treated as the offal of the world . . . the scum of the earth" (1 Cor. 4:10,13). For to live with the mind of Christ is to see the way we are to follow as a continuing and progressing emptying of ourselves, "even to death on a cross" (Phil. 2:8).

Disinterestedness does not mean that we are not interested in the task—whether this is alleviating suffering by alms or the tasks we have chosen in harmony with God's will, the responsibilities we have assumed or which simply are part of our lives. It means that we are striving to become more and more task-conscious without regard to any advantage to self, to our "feelings". It is seeing every task objectively in its relative importance, and recognized as the will of God simply because it is seen as *good*. What others will say is usually to be disregarded, unless the opinion of others affects the feasibility of a task. Obedience to peer pressure is totally incompatible with learning to live by the two great commandments—to love God, and to love as Christ loves—which contain and determine all else. "Obedience to God comes before obedience to men" (Acts 5:29). Instant yielding to pressure is rejection of the cross.

What Our Lord said about giving alms applies by implication to purity of intention in all our tasks as they are intended to be the will of God, a gift of ours, of ourselves, a service to those whom God loves—to live in humility, self-effacing, without vanity, in single-minded seeking and doing what is right. This is our constant goal, to be pursued peacefully, sought in prayer, as we try to eliminate from our lives the disastrous preoccupation with appearance, self-image, approval by others. *This looking away from ourselves must become our foremost asceticism.* "Unless you change and become like little children, you will never enter the kingdom of heaven" (Mt. 18:3) And this can only be done as we discover, in the light of faith, the realities revealed, the *content* of the faith—that we are heirs of the Fall, destined for eternal life, redeemed by the personal love of Jesus Christ, enveloping me every moment of my life. And that now, in our prayers, expiation and daily tasks we are "fellow workers of God" (1 Cor. 3:9). The remedy is a growth in our spiritual life, intelligently pursued *in* and *as* the Church. Total reality—created and uncreated—is the foundation of the moral life.

The convulsions, the cramp of the self-reflective spirit will go away as we will live *by* and *in* the realities revealed. Here is the way to liberation from the paralysis of vanity, public opinion, and preoccupation with our self-image: "if you make *my* word your home you will indeed be my disciple, you will learn the truth and the truth will make you free" (Jn. 8:31-32). And with St. Peter we will pray: "May [we] have more grace and peace as [we] *come to know our Lord more and more*". Because Our Lord Jesus Christ, "by His divine power ... has given us all the things that we need for true devotion, bringing us to *know* God himself, who has called us by His own glory and goodness" (2 Pt. 1:2-3). "Set your hearts on his kingdom first, and on his righteousness, and these other things will be given you as well" (Mt. 6:33).

Prayer in Secret

And when you pray, do not imitate the hypocrites:
they love to say their prayers standing up in the synagogues
and at the street corners for people to see them. I tell you solemnly,
they have had their reward. But when you pray, go to your private room
and, when you have shut your door, pray to your Father
who is in that secret place, and your Father who sees all
that is done in secret will reward you. (6:5-6).

Could this mean that we are to leave the world outside with its disturbing influence on our intentions, motivations, clouding our faith, misdirecting our hope, and creating the illusion that there can be charity without the cross? Could it mean that prayer of seeking God and His will in a spirit of adoration, of trusting self-effacement, could be twisted into an exercise of self-indulgence or narcissism? Is not going to our "private room", the shutting of our door, resolutely to leave the world, because "making the world [our] friend is making God [our] enemy? Anyone who chooses the world for his friend turns himself into God's enemy" (Jas. 4:4). "Pure unspoilt religion ... is ... keeping oneself uncontaminated by the world" (Jas. 1:27). Our faith, the content of which is God, His revelation of His dispositions towards us, of His ways, of His calls—all manifestations of His love—our faith, by which revelation is known and alive, "is victory over the world" (1 Jn. 5:4).

"When you pray and don't get it, it is because you have not prayed properly, you have prayed for something to indulge your own desires" (Jas. 4:3). Your prayer *will* be heard in God's own time and way, "if you remain in [Christ], and [His] words remain with you; [then] you may ask what you will and you shall get it" (Jn. 15:7). To be heard, or better, to enter into harmony with God's own plan, His own ways, His Providence, we must, according to St. James, be free from any self-indulgence affecting and distorting our desires. We must be united to Jesus. He will live in us, if we are being crucified with Him (Gal. 2:19-20). His words must have come to form our minds, we must be "rich soil", hear His word and understand it so as to yield a harvest (Mt. 13:23) towards extending and intensifying the Kingdom of God.

Such dispositions must underlie all prayer, to be, in turn, brought about through prayer, through humble listening to God, as He speaks to us in Creation, Revelation, and the circumstances of our lives, in and through the Church. "If you ask anything *in my name*, I will do it" (Jn. 14:13). We have been commissioned "to go out and bear fruit, fruit that will last; and *then* the Father will give [us] anything [we]]ask him in [Jesus'] name" (Jn. 15:16). Our prayers will become such that they *can* be heard—if we eradicate all self-indulgence, all self-seeking. We seek, in prayer, the coming of God's kingdom, "a kingdom of truth and life, . . . of holiness and grace, . . . of justice, love and peace" (Preface for the Feast of Christ the King). Nothing less can be our desire if we are to love *as* Christ loves, (Jn. 13:34), "as children of [God] that he loves, and follow Christ by loving as he loved" (Eph. 15:1-2). Only if we "seek first his kingdom and his righteousness" will all these things be ours (Mt. 6:33), will we be heard. Only then do we ask with that purity of intention without which we simply do not seek His kingdom to come. "Whatever we ask him, we shall receive, because we kept his commandments and live the kind of life that he wants" (1 Jn. 3:22). "[God] wants our desire to be exercised in prayer, thus enabling us to grasp what he is preparing to give" (from a letter of St. Augustine to Proba, reading in the Breviary for Sunday of Week 19). "The apostles' saying, 'Pray without ceasing' (1 Thes. 5:17), means nothing else but: without ceasing, desire, from him alone who can give it, the blessed life, which is none other than eternal life" (ibid). Prayer is a seeking of God, of His Way, of His will, of His kingdom—for me, for others, for all others. It is seeking for myself those dispositions that enable me to discern and enter into God's Way—to seek the Father through Him Who is this Way, the "only mediator between God and mankind, himself a man, Christ Jesus" (1 Tm. 2:5)—to pray with the desire that flows from loving as Jesus loves. It is therefore a listening to Him, the Word of the Father, to Whom we are to listen as we are told on the Mountain of Transfiguration (Mt. 17:5). If prayer is not in the service of salvation, it is unworthy, if not sacrilegious.

To become attuned to God, to acquire "the mind of Christ" (Phil. 2:5) by growing in the spirit of sacrifice, of poverty of spirit, of that kenosis which led to "death on a cross" (Phil. 2:8), is to become a willing and fit instrument of Christ. It is the necessary condition of that "spiritual revolution" that consists of putting "aside [our] old self, which gets corrupted by following illusory desires" (Eph. 4:23, 22). We are to "put on the new self that has been created in *God's* way" (Eph. 4:24). It is to rise to the new life *now*, when "the life of Christ who lives in me" finds room in me, because "I have been crucified with Christ" (Gal. 2:20, 19). All this is a mystery, it is entering into the invisible realm that we know of in faith, long for and labor for in hope, and are beginning to share by that mysterious gift of charity that "has been poured into our hearts by the Holy Spirit which has been given us" (Rom. 5:5). And this love, gift of God, shares in that "inaccessible light" of God "whom no man has seen and no man is able to see" (1 Tm. 6:16). "Now the life we have is hidden with Christ in God" (Col. 3:3).

This is why we are to go to our private room, that is, exclude all human considerations, when we wish to pray. We are to shut the door to keep out "the things that are on the earth", because our thoughts are to be "on heavenly things" (Col. 3:2). Our intention is exclusively to seek, to listen to God, and to accept His truths, His will unconditionally, without reservation, in that purity of heart which alone allows us to "see God" (Mt. 5:8).

To keep out of prayer the intrusion of the world is a life-long struggle. Distractions not only arise, but are actually sought in our escape from God, in our hiding ourselves from Him (Gn. 3:8). And when we suspect that God calls us, when we *are* beginning to recognize His holy will, excuses and rationalizing, "illusory desires" (Eph. 4:22) of the "old self", are ready to blind us again. The reality of God as the omnipotent Creator and loving, merciful Redeemer, is seen as an obstacle, as the "Other" confronting us. We must learn, by God's grace, that freedom is a gift, and that our perfection derives from God's creative power that *enables* us to believe, to hope, to love. It is *He* "who puts both the will and the action into [us]" (Phil. 2:13). Original Sin, the first rebellion, and all consequent rebellions took place, and continue to take place by man, by *me*, placing God in the role of "the other". It is more easily seen in others, or as the root of the Atheism institutionalized in the Soviet Union. It is great gain if I can discover the temptation of this kind of rebellion in my own heart, and perhaps in my yielding to it, past and present! God's love is creative, He creates in me the power to be, to grow in sanctity, to function. His love is an *enabling power*. "It is in him that we live, and move, and exist" (Acts 17:23).

In this life, we must learn from God, from His revelation in Christ Whom to see is to see the invisible God (Jn. 14:9 and Col. 1:15), to love as Christ loved (Jn. 13:34), and how this love is at work in Jesus Christ, and meant to be actualized in us by the way of the Beatitudes.

"Let [our] thoughts be on heavenly things" (Col 3:2), on Him Who is the "Light of the world" (Jn. 8:12), "not on the things that are on earth" (Col. 3:2)—for we "have no eyes for things that are visible" (2 Cor. 4:18), and therefore we "go to [our] private room . . . shut the door, pray to [our] Father who is in that secret place" (Mt. 6:6). We have eyes "only for things that are invisible" (2 Cor. 4:18). And all this because [we] have died, and now the life [we] have *is hidden with Christ in God*. But when Christ is revealed—and he is our life—[we] too will be revealed in all [our] glory with him" (Col. 3:3-4).

How to Pray: The Lord's Prayer

In your prayers do not babble as the pagans do, for they think that
by using many words they will make themselves heard. Do not be
like them; your Father knows what you need before you ask him.
So you should pray like this: "Our Father in heaven,
may your name be held holy, your kingdom come, your will be done,
on earth as in heaven. Give us today our daily bread. And forgive us
our debts, as we have forgiven those who are in debt to us.
And do not put us to the test, but save us from the evil one." (6:7-13)

St. Paul calls us "fellow workers with God" (1 Cor. 3:9), "ambassadors for Christ" (2 Cor. 5:20). We are to "bear one another's burden [Knox: failings] and so fulfill the law of Christ" (Gal. 6:2). "The Christian vocation is, of its nature, a vocation to the apostolate as well" (*Decree on the Apostolate of Lay People*, 2). These texts implement the New Commandment, that we love one another just as Christ loved us (Jn. 13:34), loved us even while He was being destroyed, as the target and victim of the sins of men, of the Sin of the World. To love as Christ loved is to share the desire of God, that His will be done, that His kingdom come, that He would be held in reverence and be adored. This desire, on our part, would mean that God's gifts—the light of faith, the hope for salvation, for sanctity, the charity that unites and flows from union—would transform us, so that God may appeal *through* us, that we—I—may become manifestation and actualization of the "mystery of God's love for men" (*Pastoral Constitution*, 45). In faith, through desire and self-effacement, my mind would become "the same as Christ Jesus" (Phil. 2:5), and God's plan would find in me a humble instrument.

Could this "mind of Christ" become mine, if I learned to pray the Our Father on behalf of others, certain others, all others? The prayer is in the plural, incorporated in the Liturgy of the Mass and the Liturgy of the Breviary. It is the Lord's Prayer, the Prayer of the Church. It is, and always should be, the prayer *of* the Church, *for* the Church, expressing the desire of the Lord Jesus, of the Church. It is the great missionary prayer, expressing, in the realization of its petitions, the purpose of Creation, the goal of Redemption, answering, articulating "a profound longing in all men" (*Decree on the Church's Missionary Activity*, 7). The Our Father expresses "the intention of the creator", which we as His "fellow workers", as His "ambassadors", must learn, must hope to be given, to share: the intention of the creator in creating man in his own image and likeness [will be] truly realized, when all who possess human nature, and have been regenerated in Christ through the Holy Spirit, gazing together on the glory of God, will be able to say 'Our Father' " (*Decree on the Church's Missionary Activity*, 7). Then "God (will) be all in all" (1 Cor. 15:28). Then his "Kingdom of truth and life . . . of holiness and grace . . . of justice, love, and peace" (Preface for the Feast of Christ the King) will have arrived, and God's will is done, without reservation, for eternity. The "bread come down from heaven" (Jn. 6:58) is now the Heart and Mediator (1 Tm. 2:5) of the Beatific Vision. Forgiveness has been given, "death is swallowed up in victory" (1 Cor. 15:55). Temptation can no longer arise in man's heart or reach it from without. Evil has been conquered with good (Rom. 12:21). "God lives among men, He will make his home among them; they shall be his people, and he will be their God . . . He will wipe away all tears from their eyes", from our eyes (Rev. 21:3-4). Faith has been transformed into seeing Him "face to face" (Rev. 22:4). Hope ceases when God's glory envelops us. Anticipation and fulfillment have become one, the love of His Who, "loved us first" (1 Jn. 4:19) finds full response in adoration and gratitude from men.

Do we not often forget the goal when we seek the *way*? Is not the (at times) paralyzing drabness of our celebrations, of our spiritual life, the effect of this lack of concrete hope, the hope for heaven as the sharing of God's glory, of His joy (Jn. 15:11; 17:13)? And may this not come from the lack of joy in people's lives, where joy has been replaced by thrills, by fun? When family life is starved by alienation between two generations who find nothing to say to one another, at best suppressing mutual irritation? Where, in human life, can the young learn of the reflections of God's gentleness, purity, generosity, and other facets of love? Do we not see how the crudeness, violence, ugliness, deteriorating language of the media, destroy the capacity for that which must serve as reflection of divine life? Has it not been a widespread, sobering disillusionment, again and again experienced, that fulfilled dreams, finally affordable, leave a void—a beautiful house, a shining car, promotion, founding a family—and now anxiety, pressures, boredom, living less and less in community, unprepared for crisis, when things dreamed of and found, are threatened? What could heaven be like, if our dreams turn out to be disappointments at best, if not burdens, presumptions having turned to emptiness of heart and mind, urging us to break out in destructive rebellion as described in Scripture: "when self-indulgence is at work [and] the results are [seen to be] obvious . . . sexual irresponsibility, idolatry . . . feuds and wrangling, jealousy, bad temper and quarrels, disagreement, factions, envy, drunkenness" (Gal. 5:19-20).

But then, the foretaste of blessedness—"love, joy, peace, patience, kindness, goodness, trustfulness, gentleness, and self-control" (Gal. 5:22)—these only the Spirit can bring us. These fruits can be ours, if our longings, our desires, are *for* God, *from* God, which only God, Creator and Redeemer, can awaken in us and fulfill. The Our Father, the "dream", or rather the revealed hope, expressed there, can guide us to those deepest desires, ultimately to God himself. If divine, revealed reality is set aside, we live without wisdom, "without hope and without God" (Eph. 2:12), "carried along by every wind of doctrine, at the mercy of all the tricks men play and their cleverness in practicing deceit" (Eph. 4:14), "corrupted by following illusory desires" (Eph. 4:22—read Eph. 4:17-24).

"If we live by the truth and in love" (Eph. 4:15), we will begin to comprehend, in faith, that God, the Creator of all, Who sustains all in existence (Heb. 1:3), is "Father", "from whom every family, whether spiritual or natural, takes its name" (Eph. 3:14-15). To us He is always the Father, waiting for our return, "moved with pity" clasping us, upon return, in his arms and kissing us tenderly (Lk. 15:20; 15:7). He is always the Father Whose glory, Whose love, Whose mercy, Whose compassion, Whose patience were seen in the Word made flesh (Jn. 1:14; 14:9). It is "the glory on the face of Christ" (2 Cor. 4:6). God's love is "made visible in Christ Jesus our Lord" (Rom. 8:39). And as *Our* Father, He is Father of *all*. His redeeming love and pity are now extended into our midst, into our hearts by Jesus Christ. Him we profess and invoke as our Redeemer, Who has excluded no one. The Father, Who lives "in inaccessible light" (1 Tm. 6:15), in heaven, comes when His seeking us (Rev. 3:19) meets with our seeking Him in Christ Jesus, the "only mediator between God and mankind, himself a man" (1 Tm. 2:5).

We learn to adore Him, we learn by doing, as we pray the Psalms and Canticles of Scripture, as we pray liturgically, applying our mind to the content of our prayers, while seeking to extend the spirit of adoration into our daily lives—we hallow His name, the Father and the Son, in the Holy Spirit. As with the Church we pray for His Kingdom, we pray implicitly that we may become fit for the Kingdom, that our capacity for God may be such that He can make His home with us (Jn. 14:23), "that Christ may live in [our] hearts through faith" (Eph. 3:17). For then we become transparent for Christ, because "we, with our unveiled faces reflecting like mirrors the brightness of the Lord, all grow brighter and brighter as we are turned into the image that we reflect" (2 Cor. 3:18). We become "ambassadors for Christ." Then God will be able to appeal through us (2 Cor. 5:20).

Condition for Being Forgiven by God

Yes, if you forgive others their failings, your heavenly Father will forgive you yours; but if you do not forgive others, your Father will not forgive your failings either. (6:14-15)

Where lies the attraction, the fascination, the pleasure of not forgiving, of sulking in small matters, of nourishing what would seem to be an illusion, that having been insulted and injured gives us power over the "enemy", even if we are made to realize by the very injury that we are powerless? Is it the satisfaction that the wrong suffered gives me rights, and if there has been wrong or sin in my life, that suffering injustice absolves me, as it were, from wrongs committed? Is the refusal to forgive, where there is repentance on the part of the wrong-doer, a form of pride springing from the primeval temptation, so fearfully alive in all of us, to "be like God, knowing good and evil" (Gn. 3:5)? The refusal to forgive, even the refusal to desire the possibility of forgiveness, might well be an acceptance of the temptation that called forth the Original Sin of our first parents—rebellion against the Creator Whose name, Love, was profoundly understood before the Fall.

The refusal to forgive when forgiveness is asked in humble repentance would seem to be destructive of our very capacity for God. How else can we understand the categorical statements in Scripture, that this refusal makes it impossible to find forgiveness from God? "If you do not forgive others, your Father will not forgive your failings either" (Jesus' words under consideration). "There will be judgment without mercy for those who have not been merciful themselves" (Jas. 2:13). The Lord's Prayer reveals that forgiveness sought depends on the willingness to grant it. And the Parable of the Unforgiving Debtor reveals the devastating effect of our own blindness with regard to the vast areas of guilt we have been forgiven, while refusal to forgive what is relatively insignificant—because injury to men is so small if compared with defiance with God. "Were you not bound to have pity on your fellow servant just as I had pity on you" (Mt. 18:33)? Is it not simply rejection of the commandments to love God if we refuse to forgive, that is, to love, where and as God loves? "Jesus Christ came into the world to save sinners" (1 Tm. 1:15). And God "wants everyone to be saved" (1 Tm. 2:4), having "imprisoned all men in their disobedience only to show mercy to all mankind" (Rom. 11:32). Moreover, who would dare to confine the prayers of the liturgies, prayed in the plural, to less than *all* human beings?

Anything less than this, any desire that certain individuals or groups should *not* receive God's blessings is the wish to undo Redemption, to reject, to crucify the Lord again and again in those whom He loves and whom we prefer to exclude. The all-pervasiveness of the refusal to forgive in family life, in political life, in relations among the peoples of the world, is the primeval and essentially destructive poison, injected by Satan, seeking to destroy God, man, all creation. Hatred, refusal to forgive, is refusal to be what we are called to be, "ambassadors for Christ" (2 Cor. 5:20). Jesus is the Redeemer of man: "God in Christ was reconciling the *world* to himself" (2 Cor. 5:19). Rigidly to contradict God's intention to save *all* is simply to contradict the Almighty Creator Whose name is Love (1 Jn. 4:8,16). It is to become uninhabitable for God Who created and redeemed us in order to dwell in us (Jn. 14:23). It is to reject the solemn prayer of Jesus that we may be one in Him and the Father, Jesus the Eternal Son in each one of us and the Father in Him (Jn. 17:22)—our union with the triune God, as we "share the divine nature" (2 Pt. 1:4).

We return once more to the pleasure, to the intoxication felt in self-righteous condemnation, nourished by having been injured, and in turn driving us more deeply into pride, wishing humiliation or destruction upon our adversary. When does this become sufficiently deliberate to make us unfit for God, thereby becoming mortal sin, fixing the heart in opposition to God, Who desires the salvation of all (1 Tm. 2:4)? In the intoxication of self-righteousness, can we still hear the fearful words of St. John, "to hate your brother is to be a murderer" (1 Jn.3:15)? Are we now ready to participate in the next Holocaust? For here may well lie the genesis of the hatreds that constituted the core of Nazism.

The feeling of power when having been wronged may well be an usurpation of power, not authority in the service of justice, but wanting to determine in sheer self-service, in rebellious independence of God, what is right and wrong—"knowing good and evil" (Gn. 3:5). If this power could dominate, it would lead to delight in the pain, in the humiliation it seeks to inflict and to perpetuate, so that the beholding of the "enemy's" agony and degradation would become an inverted, everlasting "beatific" vision.

Evil directly desired, not only willed as a means to an otherwise indifferent end or as a regrettable "necessity" in the pursuit of ordinary affairs, evil directly desired, for its own destructive sake, is the result of usurpation of the power of God, in fantasy. For what else could it be? It involves the total discarding of truth, justice, charity. It is here that Original Sin, the Fall of our first parents—continuing to be present in us as temptation—becomes a force threatening destruction. To usurp God's power is the ultimate, the most violent and destructive form of rebellion, a total flight from reality and from the Cross, where alone freedom and redemption are found. This illusion of power may be found in many forms of human relation, within marriage or between parents and children, or in the wider society.

When the categories of right and wrong, of good and evil, of love and indifference or of hate, have ceased to exist or to be understood, and only momentary feelings are recognized, contact with reality, encounter with other human beings is no longer thinkable. The criterion for good and evil have now become "*I* feel good", "*I* feel bad". Reality no longer is the foundation of morality; God becomes, if thought of at all, a projection of one's own feelings and moods. To forgive or to seek forgiveness have lost all meaning. Man is far gone on the road to final incapacity to love, to understand. Final impenitence, as a sin against hope in the form of despair or presumption, becomes a growing possibility and an eternalized fact at the moment of death. Man can fall away from truth, no longer accepting truth as binding, rather directing his life to the destruction of truth. Man's spirit may become diseased when he denies the seriousness of love and bases his life upon calculation, force and deceit. Only by transcending the mainly descriptive achievements of social sciences, and becoming again radically judgmental, seeing human reality again in the light of faith, can we resist the enormous and growing pressures of the diseased spirit of the world. Only thus can we recognize the will to ultimate destruction of the human spirit sought by communism and other totalitarianisms. Their leaders are not simply gangsters active in politics. The battle is for men's souls.

In the life of each one of us, refusal to forgive because of the (imagined) power it gives us over the offender, the playing of God in wrath expecting servile submission of the offender, this can become a force irreversible by man alone. Total conversion is the only hope. This kind of self-righteousness may lead to something resembling paranoia and to a complete loss of the sense of reality. Only the grace of God, God's creative, transforming power, can penetrate this darkness, this blindness of a diseased spirit. When God speaks to us, we will not hear His voice, because our hearts have become hardened (Psalm 95). But should the light begin to penetrate the darkness and delusion of self-righteousness, we must begin to pray, "I believe; help my unbelief" (Mt. 9,24).

Fasting in Secret

When you fast do not put on a gloomy look as the hypocrites do:
they put on long faces to let men know they are fasting. I tell you solemnly,
they have had their reward. But when you fast, put oil on your head
and wash your face, so that no one will know you are fasting
except your Father who sees all that is done in secret; and your Father
who sees all that is done in secret will reward you. (6:16-18)

This instruction of our Lord is more than the establishment of an exercise of the ascetic life, that when fasting we are to forego the satisfaction of being seen, admired and praised. Besides practicing self-denial of food, we are to disassociate ourselves from the two always present temptations—to behold ourselves with satisfaction because we are winning a contest; and to seek approval, to serve our image. Cultivating both, the so-called self-image and the external image—seeing ourselves fasting, and being seen fasting—undo the purpose and meaning of the spiritual life: setting our "hearts on [God's] kingdom *first*, and on his righteousness" (Mt. 6:33) on His holiness, to seek and serve God unconditionally. Cultivating one's image is a denial of reality and undermining the seeking of God's will and kingdom, for which we are told to pray in the Our Father.

What Our Lord said about almsgiving, "not to parade [our] good deeds before men to attract their notice" (Mt. 6:1), holds for fasting, for all visible aspects of our seeking God. We are to set ourselves against an all-pervasive ideal of life in our times, the pre-occupation with "image," self-image, and the image presented to the world. Both tendencies are destructive of truth, lead to illusion, and undermine our spiritual life.

First, the idea of "image" implies that there need not be harmony between appearance and reality. It opens the door for deception, which is lying—to oneself, to others. Make-believe, staging oneself, calculating the effect one produces, is a form of manipulation. It destroys truth between people. Language, dress, motions, gestures, facial expressions—they become instruments of hiding and game-playing. Have we gone too far in interpreting Christ's injunction to hide our fasting, our mortifications? Or should we see in Christ's teaching, which simply expresses His [and His Mother's] essentially hidden life and apostolate, something of broad application, particularly vital in our age where cultivating images is so common in public life, and extends now even to the once unself-conscious young. It affects our spiritual life, our seeking and finding of God, shifts guilt feelings from sin to the staining of our image, from reality to shadows. In a manner that is really not very subtle, the standards of the world usurp the ways of God, and sin becomes violating what *men* tell us is important. How often do we hear the phrase "this is very important to me". It is pre-occupation and pursuit of "finding one's life" rather than "losing one's life" for the sake of Our Lord Jesus Christ (Mt. 11:39). It is rejection of the cross without which we cannot follow Him (Mt. 11:38). It is to exchange "the glory of the immortal God with the worthless imitation, for the image of mortal men" (Rom. 1:23). It is refusing, in yielding to the pressures of the world, to "learn to be a fool 'for the sake of Christ' " (1 Cor. 3:18; 4:10) to become receptive to the wisdom of God, of the crucifixion of the Son of God, Jesus Christ, the Lord—"illogical to those who are not on the way to salvation" (1 Cor. 1:18).

As destructive as the cultivation of an image to be seen by others is pre-occupation with the self, with the self-image. It has become an obsession upsetting and distorting our perception, and our thinking of God, of the very content of our faith, of what is revealed for our salvation. This pre-occupation is playing havoc with our spiritual life. It destroys our peace, it drains our nervous energy. It may replace perception of, and sorrow for, our sins with guilt feelings where there is no question of guilt before God. At times this gives us the comfortable feeling of being true penitents. it leads to emptiness of life and mindlessness, further confirmed by the spread of substitutes for reality, cosmetics, wigs, gruesome funeral customs, C. B. Radio, home computers without serious purpose, vast expenditures for cameras, video games, and time-devouring all-present television.

If fasting, prayer, liturgical life, the Mass are to be understood as real and relating to ultimate reality, to the Living God, Creator and Redeemer, we cannot seek and find Him for the sake of being seen. We either lead religious lives to serve God, or we go through the motions to serve our self-image, to feed our illusions about ourselves. But to live alone with our self image will soon become a desire to impress others with our religious pursuits and all-too-visible achievements. We "will keep up the outward appearance of religion but will have rejected the inner power of it" (2 Tm. 3:5). Certain fearful words of the Lord may then be addressed to me: "You who are like whitewashed tombs that look handsome on the outside, but inside are full of dead men's bones and every kind of corruption" ... appearing "from the outside like good honest men, but inside ... full of hypocrisy and lawlessness" (Mt. 23:27-28). Those thus addressed by Our Lord were soon to succeed in crucifying Him.

Today, possibly more than ever before, the danger of losing sight of reality, and with it, losing sight of the Creator, is an almost inescapable threat, as the means of escaping reality intrude everywhere into our lives, while there is little in us to resist, as we yield to manipulation.

We do not know whether tribulations before the end of the world, as predicted by Our Lord (Mt. 24, 4-14) are approaching, or whether they have a prelude in countries once Christian. We are not to know (Mt. 24:36), we are to stay awake, "because [we] do not know the day when the master is coming" (Mt. 24:42). But we must hold ourselves ready, not only for death (Mt. 25:1-13), but for the time when "love in most men will grow cold" (Mt. 24:12), when "false Christs and false prophets will arise and produce great signs and portents, enough to deceive even the chosen, if that were possible" (Mt. 24:24).

To grow in single-minded fidelity to God and to the Vicar of the Risen Christ is the only hope, the only way. And this implies at the present day a spirit, an attitude of obedience that is free of human respect, does not yield to peer pressure, is free of vanity, discerns what is of God, what of man. This can only grow in us as the truth makes us free (Jn. 8:12). This freedom means that we are firmly rooted in the revealed fact that "nothing can . . . come between us and the love of Christ . . . between us and the love of God made visible in Christ Jesus our Lord" (Rom. 8:35, 39). Today seduction away from the faith, away from the Church is offered in the name of compassion. Abortion, contraception, contraceptive sterilization, euthanasia are advocated in this name of compassion, so that by opposing them our image is liable to be stained. We appear as merciless. We are called to the hidden martyrdom of complete misunderstanding, following Him Who let "himself be taken for a sinner, while he was bearing the faults of many and praying all the time for sinners" (Is. 53:12). Our life, in post Christian society will be a hidden life, because [we] have died, and now the life [we] have is hidden with Christ in God" (Col. 3:3-4). When one cannot be certain whether some priest or Bishop, some Superior, some administration *called* Catholic *is* Catholic, persecution within the Church will become more frequent. A great deal of this is commonplace in the United States, hidden under slick doubletalk, sounding ironic, yet deadly. The victims are called to a degree of "emptying themselves" that may well be prepared for by fasting, by mortifications and a rigorous application of the intelligence in prayer (to love God with all our *mind*—Mk. 12:30), while remaining hidden. The warnings of Our Lord are meant for us, because the "last days" are preparing with growing intensity and seductive power.

Trying to live by the absolute priority of God and to be available to God as His "fellow workers" (1 Cor. 3:9; 2 Cor. 5:18-20) in bringing salvation to earth, as members of the Risen Lord, Who possesses "all authority in heaven and on earth" (Mt. 28:18), we live by the Great Commandment to love God unconditionally. We give Him all our heart, all our soul, all our *mind* (intelligence, illuminated by the content of the faith), all our strength (Mk. 12:30). And we love one another as Jesus Christ has loved us (Jn. 13:34), "obedient unto death, even death on a cross" (Phil. 2:8). The kingdom of God requires total self-efface-ment, generosity, a complete divesting of self: Poverty of Spirit. And we must be ready to suffer persecution (Mt. 5:3, 10). "Jesus too suffered outside the gate to sanctify the people with his own blood. Let us go to Him, then, outside the camp, and share his degradation" (Heb. 13:12-13).

V

Providence

True Treasures

Do not store up treasures for yourselves on earth,
where moths and woodworms destroy them and thieves can break in
and steal. But store up treasures for yourselves in heaven,
where neither moth nor woodworms destroy them
and thieves cannot break in and steal. For where your treasure is,
there will your heart be also. (6:19-21)

The principle theme of the first two chapters of Genesis is that the world and man are created, that is, willed by God; that man is the crown of creation, for whom creation exists, that he may "have dominion . . . over all the earth . . . [to] be fruitful and multiply, and fill the earth and subdue it" (Gn. 1:26,28). He is created to have dominion, to subdue, but also to discover the marvels of creation and to adore Him Who willed it and Whose creative word forms it and maintains it in being and functioning (Jn. 1:3; Col. 1:15-17; Heb. 1:3). Through man's rebellion, Original Sin, God had made creation "unable to attain its purpose" (Rom. 8:20). "Creation still retains the hope of being freed" (Rom. 8:20). All creation is "groaning in one great act of giving birth" (Rom. 8:22), while Christians—those "called to be fellow workers with God" (1 Cor. 3:9)—have to "go through the pain of giving birth . . . until Christ is formed" in all (Gal. 4:19).

Man, wounded deeply by the original rebellion, and wounding himself again and again by sin, possesses a mysterious relation to the world, which has been entrusted to him (Gn. 1:26). He is at present discovering how greatly he is wasting and abusing it by technologies that often are developed and applied without wisdom, under delusions of greed, power and pride, that may well become suicidal in their eventual destruction of intelligence. Resentment of God and His reflection in man—holiness—led to the first murder (Gn. 4:4-7), made men kill the prophets (Mt. 5:12; 23:34) and continues to torment the just, for "a servant is not greater than his master" (Jn. 15:20). To exclude God and His reflections from one's life—justice (Acts 7:52), truth (Jn. 14:6), charity (1 Jn. 4:8,16)—is to "store up treasures . . . on earth", to become increasingly self-serving, even under the guise of serving God, as many of the Pharisees did. "The hour is coming when anyone who kills you will think he is doing a holy duty for God" (Jn. 16:2). It may be done in ignorance, as was the case with St. Paul before his conversion (1 Tm. 1:13). Thus the repeated spectacle of Christians fighting each other, many in invincible ignorance of the full truth.

It is not too difficult to consider and observe ways of storing up treasures on earth, the ways of what Our Lord called "the world". But *His* kingdom was, is, not "of this world" (Jn. 18:36). We are not to model ourselves "on the behavior of the world around [us]" (Rom. 12:2). "The wisdom of this world is foolishness to God" (1 Cor. 3:19). That "the world", that is, human affairs under the power of sin, can enter the life of the Church is only too plain. Peter already was told that the way he thought was "not God's way but man's" (Mt. 16:23).

We are considering a profound mystery when we try to speak of "treasures . . . in heaven" where our heart ought to be. It is not here a question of longing for heaven, "the glory as yet unrevealed, which is waiting for us" which, in its intensity and eternity, is incommensurable with the sufferings of this life (Rom. 8:18). We could not consider ourselves Christians if heaven, as the promise and goal of human existence, is not central to the realities revealed that constitute the content of our faith and of our hope. Here it is a question, not of the reward, God Himself, Whom we are to see "face to face" (Rv. 22:4), sharing "the divine nature" (2 Pt. 1:4). What could be meant by the treasures *we* are to store up for ourselves?

As we are called, and enabled to become, "light of the *world*" (Mt. 5:14), in our own resurrection we should become lights in heaven, continuing there to illuminate the Blessed. Man's perfection becomes an element of eternal glory. Everything that contributed to holiness, everything that was done and accomplished in the spirit of generosity, of self-giving, with the dispositions which God can, and does, transform into charity will enter *through* me, *in* me, *as* me, into eternity. For nothing truly good is ever lost, except through final impenitence. On earth, "the light shed by the Good News of the glory of Christ, who is the image of God" (2 Cor. 4:4) transforms us, to the extent of our capacity for generosity and self-effacement, into "children of light", with the effect of the light seen "in complete goodness and right living and truth" (Eph. 5:9). "The brightness of the Lord", seen face to face, will turn us "into the image that we reflect . . . the work of the Lord who is Spirit" (2 Cor. 3:18). We men become Christ-like in accord with our personality in its human perfection, its specific talents, and lasting achievements that have had their impact on the "unity in the work of service, building up the body of Christ" (Eph. 4:12).

If we have lived "by the truth and in love", having grown "in all ways into Christ, who is the head by whom the whole body is fitted and joined together, *every joint adding its own strength* (Eph. 4:15-16), we have "become the perfect Man, fully mature with the fullness of Christ himself" (Eph. 4:13). Then creation, "the universe itself, which is so closely related to man and *which attains its destiny through him,* will be perfectly reestablished in Christ (Eph. 1:10)" (*Dogmatic Constitution,* 48). Man, carrying in his very being all his true achievements, now transfigured by God and seen in their total context of origin and effect, man is now eternally alive, glorified, transfigured, as member of the Body of Christ into which we have been built up, "in love" (Eph. 4:16).

The task and the testing of our obedience to the Command to love God (Mk. 12:29-30) is the fidelity of our love of neighbor, patterned after Jesus' love for us, a love maintained by Him while being rejected (Jn. 13:34; Lk. 23:34; Jn. 12:32; 2 Tm. 2:13). An obedient longing, tested in the circumstances of our life, to follow Jesus, is the "seeking" necessary to "find". Prayer is the "asking" necessary to be given access to the kingdom, to become accessible for the kingdom, to become fit for the indwelling of the Triune God. "Knocking at the door" is necessary to be admitted (Mt. 7:7), all in response to the enabling, creative power of Him Who already stands at the door, knocking (Rev. 3:20)—God begging!

As faith, hope and charity lay hold of more and more of our lives, of our thoughts, actions, resignations, crosses, as our relations to God and neighbor are being transformed by the wisdom of God, of the God Who emptied Himself even to death on a cross (Phil. 2:8), all these become treasures we store up in heaven. They all put their stamp on our personality. In us they will be transfigured *in, as* the glory of heaven, glorifying for ever the Creator and Redeemer. The humblest human activity, if done in obedience—that is, out of love for God—creates a treasure for heaven to enter heaven by my resurrection. Their effect on others here on earth, usually hidden on earth, becomes in *them,* when risen, a treasure in heaven. This affects every genuine human activity, if the prevailing intentions flow from truth possessed in faith, from longing which is hope, from generosity in self-effacing self-giving which is the human, God-given, condition for the super-natural gift of charity. These three, faith, hope and charity, illuminate and perfect one another, and are fertile in the "building up of the body of Christ" (Eph. 4:12) as others are illuminated and turn "into light" (Eph. 5:14), as the uncreated light that transfigures the Risen Lord and, in shining *on* me, shines *through* me—"it is as though God were appealing through us" (2 Cor. 5:20).

When works of genius are drawn into this transfiguration of creation—*through* men, *in* men, *for* men—preparation of "a way for the Lord, making his paths straight" by a "voice crying in the wilderness" (Mt. 3:3) takes place. It is the preparation of the "rich soil" for "the word of the kingdom" that will yield a rich harvest (Mt. 13:23,18). This has been, for example, the function of art in clothing the Liturgy of the Church. Self-effacing service, often anonymous, produced tangible manifestations and actualizations of "the mystery of God's love for men" (*Pastoral Constitution*, 45). Thus art and the artists had an essential part in the incarnation of divine truth, of divine life in men and society, which would finally become, *in* and *through* their influence on men, treasures in heaven. All true art, not only when in the service of divine worship, prepares the way for God. How desperately deprived is the present generation, drowned in trash designed to destroy the human spirit, trash which all too frequently overflows even into divine service!

By contrast, great art, great music shares in the sacramental vocation of men—to reveal God, to be the instrument of God. And in this way treasures are stored up in heaven, anchoring our hearts where our treasures are, where these treasures have borne fruit. Nor is greatness necessary. The sufferings of men in seeking beauty, as in seeking goodness, are seeds from which much beauty, much glory in the New Heaven and the New Earth will spring. Whether hidden or visible, whether confined to man's hearts or visible to others, no true achievement ever perishes or remains without fruit. Creation, once fallen, will be liberated and reach heaven in and through men. The love of God "made visible in Christ Jesus our Lord" (Rom. 8:39) now seeks all men, and *through* and *in* them enters the New Jerusalem.

"Then I heard a voice from heaven say to me, 'Write down: Happy are those who die in the Lord! Happy indeed, the Spirit says; now they can rest forever after their work, *since their good deeds go with them*' " (Rv. 14:13). And these, together with their everlasting effects, are the treasures we have stored up for ourselves in heaven.

The Eye, the Lamp of the Body

The lamp of the body is the eye. It follows that if your eye is sound,
your whole body will be filled with light. But if your eye is diseased,
your whole body will be darkness. If then, the light inside you
is darkness, what darkness that will be! (6:22-23)

How can the light inside us be darkness (Mt. 6:23)? Can it happen that we meet Jesus Christ, hear His words, learn of His death and resurrection, can it happen that He, the "Light of the World" (Jn. 8:12), actually shines into our hearts, but that we "prefer darkness to the light because [our] deeds [are] evil" (Jn. 3:19)? Could we come to hate the light and avoid it, for fear our actions should be exposed (Jn. 3:20)?

In the words of the Lord which we are trying to consider, would "the eye" be the ability to be illuminated by the light, that we may become "light in the Lord, . . . children of light" (Eph. 5:9)? This happens when "the *effects* of the light" are allowed, in our freedom, to become "complete goodness and right living and truth" (Eph. 5:9). Then "the eye is sound," our whole being will be filled with the light (Mt. 6:22). Then we will be illuminated and turn into light (Eph. 5:14). We have made contact with "the fountain of *life*," in whose light we see light (Ps. 36:9).

The eye for divine reality is the ability for "seeing the light shed by the Good News of the glory of Christ, Who is the image of God" (2 Cor. 4:4). For it is God the Creator Who said, " 'Let there be light shining out of darkness,' who has shone in our minds to radiate the light of the knowledge of God's glory, the glory on the face of Christ" (2 Cor. 4:6). Blessed is the eye which can perceive God's glory in the humanity of the eternal Son, in Jesus Christ, the "only mediator between God and mankind, Himself a man, Christ Jesus" (1 Tm. 2:5). Here lies the key to the whole Gospel—"to have seen Me is to have seen the Father" (Jn. 14:9)—the key without which Jesus, Revelation, Scripture, the Mystery of the Church, the mystery and destiny of man, remain isolated and do not converge into one light which we see and by which we see. Thus if "the light inside [us] is darkness" (Mt. 6:23), it is fatal. "He who rejects Me and refuses My words has his judge already: the word itself that I have spoken will be his judge on the last day" (Jn. 12:48). The lost light becomes a kind of dynamic darkness, possessing living human beings, which will seek to expand the darkness, led on by "Sovereignties and Powers, who originate the darkness in this world" (Eph. 6:12). There is a "faith" that turns light received into destructive darkness, falsehood, ignorance, hatred. "The demons believe and they tremble with fear" (Jas. 2:19). That may be related to that frightening phenomenon when a believer, turning away from his faith, from "Jesus, the pioneer and perfecter of our faith" (Heb. 12:2), seeks to destroy the faith in men's hearts, disguising himself "as sheep but underneath [he is] a ravenous wolf" (Mt. 7:15).

"To have seen Me is to have seen the Father" (Jas. 14:9). The Father lives in inaccessible light (1 Tm. 6:16), He Who is, "origin without origins," Who is fullness, holiness, creative power, gentleness, humility, justice, compassion. He is eternally Father, begetting His likeness or Son, and the Love which—better, *Who*—is the dynamism of this eternal generation and self-giving, the Holy Spirit. He is one God, one Divine

Nature, three Persons, one in Substance with one another. This is an ineffable, inaccessible, yet now accessible, mystery, of Him in Whom "we live, and move and exist" (Acts 17:28). Him we see in Jesus, as Jesus' life unfolds from conception to Lordship and toward the consummation of the divine venture of creation, when "the Son Himself will be subject in His turn to the One Who subjected all things to Him, so that God may be all in all" (1 Cor. 15:28).

The eternal Son, through Whom "all things came to be" (Jn. 1:3), communicated His glory to His assumed humanity, so that in Jesus can be perceived "the glory that is His as the only Son of the Father, full of grace and truth" (Jn. 1:14). The eternal Image, Likeness, Word, Son, of the Father, unseen in His Godhead, became the *visible* image by Incarnation (Col. 1:15).

The believer knows reality, and himself, not only *willed* by God, but himself *loved*. He knows, in faith and hope, that "God loved the world so much, that He gave His only Son, so that everyone . . . may have eternal life" (Jn. 3:16). He now knows that "God is Love" (1 Jn. 4, 8, 16), Redeemer, that nothing "can ever come between us and the love of God *made visible in Jesus Christ Our Lord*" (Rom. 8:39). This transfiguration in creation, of man, of man's hope, happens when we live by the truth, by the light that is Love, and come to perceive the Father when we come to know Jesus, the "light of the World" (Jn. 8:12). He is "the true light that enlightens all men" (Jn. 1:9). It is a light shining into the hearts and consciences of all men, accepted by some, rejected by others, in ways hidden from men. Vatican II speaks of "those who, without any fault of theirs, have not yet arrived at an explicit knowledge of God, and who, not without grace, strive to lead a good life. Whatever good or truth is found amongst them is considered by the Church to be a preparation for the Gospel and given by Him Who enlightens all men that they may at length have life" (*Dogmatic Constitution*, 16). Thus there is some divine light everywhere, and the "eye," if illuminated, enables men to perceive divine reality clothed in human words, in signs of this world. A hidden longing lives in all hearts, a deep discontent with self, yet a hope, however dim. This secret pattern, preparation for the Gospel, can be stifled, but it may expand and allow grace to produce fruit. Certainly, there are tremendous treasures of goodness, of holiness among non-Christians, waiting to become articulated by the light of the Gospel.

God's "everlasting power and deity" (Rom. 1:20) should be perceived and welcomed by all. All men are enlightened by the Word (Jn. 1:9). Some accept it in the deep recesses of the heart, others hate the light and avoid it (Jn. 3:20). God alone knows the hearts of men (1 Sam.

16:7). With this perception of God's power and deity and of our loss of innocence, there arises a hope for delivery. Even if these perceptions remain vague, are not articulated, are not confirmed by the light of revelation, they provide a light that enables man to live and to seek, free of presumption and despair. And to seek is already to have found and an infallible way of finding (Mt. 7:7), in God's own time and way, always in the resurrection.

The "eye is sound" (Mt. 6:22) if existence speaks to us of an "everlasting power and deity," if we do not let ourselves be imprisoned by the gross materialism that excludes all wonder, all seeking for *given* meaning. But it is so convenient to rationalize our selfishness, pride, greed, power sought in pride and vanity, and the flood of evil springing from these that brings incalcuable suffering into the world. Then the light shining into the heart is turned into darkness (Mt. 6:23). "If then, the light inside you is darkness what darkness that will be" (Mt. 6:23). But "if your eye is sound, your whole body," your whole being, "will be filled with light" (Mt. 6:22). It will be a life of illuminating faith, by the light of the glorious content of the Faith. It will be a life of hope, free from presumption, pride, despondency and despair, knowing by a living faith that "what we suffer in this life can never be compared to the glory, as yet unrevealed, which is waiting for us" (Rom. 8:18). It will be a life of love, thereby extending the redeeming love of God into a world of confusion, despair and mad presumption. And, without realizing it, we will be "innocent and genuine, perfect children of God among a deceitful and underhand brood, and [we] will shine in the world like bright stars" (Phil. 2:15).

God and Money

*No man can serve two masters; for either he will hate the one
and love the other; or he will be devoted to the one
and despise the other. You cannot serve God and mammon. (6:24)*

Mammon, money, and all that money can buy—flattery, respect, power, submission, pleasures, fame, positions, satisfactions of sensual desires, and any blending of these—all these can only be pursued by gradually moving away from the knowledge and service of God, the Creator and Redeemer, Whose Name is Love (1 Jn. 4:8, 16). "The Lord your God is a devouring fire, a jealous God" (Dt. 4:24). The statement we are considering is an application of the truth, of the fact that God is God, Creator of all, without Whose creative thought and creative will nothing can exist or function, as He sustains "the universe by His powerful command" (Heb. 1:3). "For us there is one God, the Father, *from Whom* all things come and *for Whom* we exist" (1 Cor. 8:6).

The "member of one of the leading families," when called by the Son of God to sell all and give the money to the poor, "when he heard this ... was filled with sadness, for he was very rich" (Lk. 18:22-23). "How hard it is for those who have riches to make their way into the kingdom of God" (Lk. 18:24). We cannot have other gods before Him—the first Commandment (Dt. 5:7), of which the other nine are but implementations. It may well be said that the measure of perfection, if we could measure it in this life, is the extent to which we really mean the words "Thy kingdom come, Thy will be done," because the price for the kingdom, the way to the kingdom, is the energetic, fearless seeking and doing of His will. To do this unconditionally *is* perfection. But then, only the Handmaid of the Lord could say with the unconditional, total trust, in a flawless interplay with faith, hope and thoroughly mature charity, "be it done according to Your word" (Lk. 1:38). And then, the Word could become flesh and dwell among us, so we could see in a human being bearing her features "the glory that is His as the only Son of the Father, full of grace and truth' (1 Jn. 1:14). Because of her word we are now able to discern "the knowledge of God's glory, the glory on the face of Christ" (2 Cor. 4:6), a face possessing a family resemblance to that of His Mother.

But the Blessed Lord did not implement His teaching on the incompatibility of God and mammon by describing the corruption of greed, of avarice, of the vices nourished by these—pride, vanity, the irresponsible use of power. He spoke of the beauty of creation as it springs from the hand of God. And yet, there are the crying injustices pervading the world, the ruthlessness of men everywhere, the ever increasing number of lawsuits in the United States, the cynical exploitation of the weak and the consequent torrents of suffering everywhere, broken homes, growing rejection of children among the wealthy, morality in public life confined to rhetoric. Is "justice" the principle concern, when decisions are to be made? And is it not a cheap and widespread deception, and quite successful, to play up capitalism as the *only* alternative to Marxism? We must not lightly ignore the prophetic voices of the past. We must listen to the voices of the Vicars of Christ, as during the last hundred years they have spoken to the world. For the Church is "the oracle of God," as Newman said. Is the bankruptcy of human wisdom not clear, as the cry of the tortured reaches us? Tortured by hunger, by constant humiliations, by boredom, by merciless bureaucracies, by the despair induced in presenting abortion as a necessary remedy which is equivalent to proclaiming the bankruptcy of God and His ways. We have not seen the full effect of declaring the bankruptcy of God's ways as we seek solutions to problems by directly defying God by mass killing of the unborn. "The wisdom of this world is foolishness to God" (1 Cor 3:19). Chesterton told us that Christianity has not failed; it has not been tried. But to try it is to acquire the mind of Christ as revealed by the Lord in His gentleness, humility (Mt. 11:29) and vulnerability, and described by St. Paul as an emptying of the Son of God even unto death on a cross (Phil. 2:5-8). We must "set our hearts on *His* kingdom first, and on His justice (holiness), and all these other things will be given [us] as well" (Mt. 6:33). Our "mind must be renewed by a spiritual revolution so that [we] can put on the new self that has been created in God's way, in the goodness and holiness of the truth" (Eph. 4:23-24). Simple words, but if really heard, if falling on "rich soil" (Mt. 13:23), and only then, they will open up into the infinite splendour of the Creator Whose name is Love, shining through the humanity that is His in which we continue to see that glory which belongs to Him "as the only Son of the Father, full of grace and truth" (Jn. 1:14). For thereby He *is* the Truth, the Life we are to share, the way into the Heart of the Triune God, and our baptismal Resurrection (Jn. 14:6; 11:25) which will become irrevocable at the moment of death.

The simple words of Our Lord we are considering place before us the choice our life is to be—God or mammon, eternal life or eternal resentment, the wisdom of the Cross or the oppressive stench of willed stupidity, which is the preferred distortion and destruction of truth.

And yet, these and similar considerations do not answer the questions of so many earnest people, what they are to do, how to know when temporal concerns are valid, whether more money or time should be given to God, to the poor, where self-denial is God's will or illusion, how much sacrifice to impose on the family. When does preoccupation with one's self-image destroy the capacity for love, which is obedience to the *commands* to love God (Mk. 12:30) and neighbor (Jn. 13:34)? What is the will of God for me *now*? To the Rich Young Man Our Lord said, "Sell all that you own and distribute your money among the poor" (Lk. 18:22). He did not ask this of St. Thomas More, who found himself, somewhat unexpectedly, a Martyr, having to give all. He was ready; the Rich Young Man was not. Everyone's vocation is different. It is *my* task to hear His voice, not to harden my heart (Ps. 94:8). It is to live by the God-given powers and abilities of faith, hope and charity—discerning God's truths, His promises and Him as a source of love, Who has loved us first (1 Jn. 4:19).

No easy answer can be given to the question of how to discover God's will in the details of life. It is the application of the two great commandments, to love God, and to love each other as Christ loved, and loves, and the many instructions found in Scripture implementing these, as the mind of Christ is formed in us. It is the life of emptying oneself, to become a servant (Phil. 2:1-8), to accept the crosses found in life (Mt. 10:37-39). It is to be a life rooted in prayer and expiation. It is to "set [our] hearts on [God's] kingdom first, and on His holiness" (Mt. 6:33). It is to entrust ourselves to the Church. And as the mind of Christ, imperceptibly, comes to transform our selfishness into a spirit of poverty and generosity, we will come to realize what God wants of us, because by the powers of a growing and purified faith, hope and charity, temptations will be discerned, and the strength to overcome will be ours by the grace of God Who alone puts the enabling will and action into us (Phil. 2:13). But at this moment of history, we must, above all, place our *intelligence* into the service of God, we must love Him "with all our mind" (Mk. 12:30)—this is the divine command! We must work hard to come to an even deeper understanding of the content of the Faith, of the unseen realities revealed, with the aid of the Church—Scripture, liturgical texts, the Church's solemn teaching in Professions of Faith, in Councils, in Papal Teaching, in the writings of the great and authentic doctors, past and recent, given to us by Divine Providence. The Church, in Vatican II, summarizes it: "*Only* by the *light of faith* and by *meditation on the word of God* can one always and everywhere recognize God in Whom 'we live and move, and have our being' (Acts 17:28), see His will in every event, see Christ in all men whether they be close to us or strangers, and make correct judgements about the true meaning and value of temporal things, both in themselves and in their relation to man's final goal" (*Decree on the Apostolate of the Laity*, 4).

Christian existence is totally rooted in the realities revealed—the Triune God, Incarnation, Redemption, Church, man as heir of Original Sin yet loved by God Who "with enduring love takes pity on us" (Is. 54:8), Who "wants everyone to be saved" (1 Tm. 2:4).

We will have to learn that God's ways are not our ways (Is. 55:8), that "God's foolishness is wiser than human wisdom, and God's weakness is stronger than human strength" (1 Cor 1:25) We must realize that more than ever, Christ Crucified is madness to the world (1 Cor. 2:23), that Jesus Christ and those who seek to be His followers will be "a sign that is rejected" (Lk. 2:34). We cannot attain to a realistic view of God's will in our lives unless, with St. Paul, we have the courage to be "fools for the sake of Christ" (1 Cor 4:10), and are willing to be "treated as the offal of the world, still to this day, the scum of the earth" (1 Cor. 4:13). In our image-conscious culture this requires quite some departure.

"How rich are the depths of God—how deep His wisdom and knowledge—and how impossible to penetrate His motives or understand His methods! Who could ever know the mind of the Lord? Who could ever be His counsellor? Who could ever give Him anything or lend Him anything? All that exists comes from Him; all is by Him and for Him. To Him be glory forever! Amen" (Rom. 11:33-36).

Trust in Providence

That is why I am telling you not to worry about your life and what you are to eat, nor about your body and how you are to clothe it. Surely life means more than food, and the body more than clothing! Look at the birds in the sky. They do not sow or reap or gather into barns; yet your heavenly Father feeds them. Are you not worth more than they are? Can any of you, for all his worrying, add one single cubit to his span of life? And why worry about clothing? Think of the flowers growing in the fields; they never have to work or to spin; yet I assure you not even Solomon in all his regalia was robed like one of these. Now if that is how God clothes the grass in the field which is there today and thrown into the furnace tomorrow, will he not much more look after you, you men of little faith? So do not worry; do not say, 'What are we to eat? What are we to drink? How are we to be clothed?' It is the pagans who set their hearts on all these things. Your heavenly Father knows you need them all. Set your hearts on His kingdom first, and on His righteousness, and all these other things will be given you as well. So do not worry about tomorrow; tomorrow will take care of itself. Each day has enough trouble of its own. (6:25-34)

"All things that He founded, God by His providence protects and governs, 'reaching from end to end mightily and governing all things well' (Wis. 8:1). 'For all things are naked and open to his eyes' (Heb. 4:13), even those things which are future by the free action of creatures" (Vatican I). Thus teaches the Church about Divine Providence. The reality of this providence is contained in our profession of the fact that God is the Father, that He is almighty, Creator of all. It is contained in our profession that God is "He Who is, as He revealed to Moses; and [that] He is Love, as the Apostle John teaches us; so that these two names, Being and Love, express ineffably the same divine Reality of Him Who has wished to make Himself known to us, and

Who 'dwelling in light inaccessible,' is in Himself above every name, above everything" (*Credo of the People of God*, Pope Paul VI). This we believe, this faith we maintain in spite of all the apparent contradictions the world of man and of nature presents to us. Evil and suffering obscure, even hide, the true face of God, the face of His loving providence. "Truly, God of Israel, the Savior, You are a God Who lies hidden" (Is. 45:15).

St. Paul wrote that "ever since God created the world His everlasting power and deity—however invisible—have been there for the mind to see in the things he has made" (Rom. 1:20). In the words we are considering Our Lord points to the *beauty* of creation, to the wonders of the flight of birds, the beauty of flowers—revelations not only of God's intelligence supremely shown in the functioning of nature, but in the splendor of His creation willed for the sake of men, a revelation of His glory drawing forth everlasting praise from the blessed.

But human life is infinitely more precious. We are made for eternal bliss, to see God face to face. We are of *this* world that is entrusted to us (Gen. 1:28), but each of us is also spirit, naturally indestructible, and called to union with God, to be partaker of the divine nature. He has "called us *by*" and *to* "His own glory and goodness" (2 Pt. 1:4, 3). "What we suffer in this life can never be compared to the glory as yet unrevealed, which is waiting for us" (Rom. 8:18).

Creation, humanity, would be a cruel joke, an outrageous absurdity if there were not some blessedness meant for *all*, attainable for *all*, essentially independent of natural gifts of body and spirit. The injustices of this world would confront us with equally unacceptable choices—either God is indifferent, callous, and therefore evil, or there is no transcendent source of existence. There is only *one* alternative to these two nightmares—that the qualities of justice and love, of possible mercy and the will to see equity restored belong to the Source of all, Who somehow would also be the goal of creation *through* man. But would such conclusion of human reasoning alone not be the height of presumption? Would one not, by the mere force of such wild conclusion, have to show a willingness to have no share in the injustices of the world? Would one not have to live, in reckless abandon, without much support from others by the great teaching of Socrates, that it is better to suffer wrong than to do wrong? Who is wise and strong enough to face the mockery, the loneliness, the persecutions and failures such a life will bring? Socrates was given hemlock to drink.

Creation reveals the Creator to all (Rom. 1:20). The absurdity of excluding the very possibility of a formative mind and will *because* we are discovering causes and purposes in nature, is mysterious and seems to point to the influence of an evil seducer—the Prince of this world. He would later put into the mind of Judas to betray Him Who *is* Truth (Jn. 14:6)—betray Him with a kiss (Lk. 22:47-48). The kiss continues to be given when destruction and prevention, exploitation and degradation of human life today are proposed (and enforced) under the guise (or pretense) of compassion. Human sacrifice is back, not from fear of evil powers, but in the service of a utopia none of those now living will enjoy.

But where is God? Is it still possible to speak of Divine Providence? Where can we begin to bridge the contradiction between the omnipotence of God Whose name is Love, and the success of evil, the universality of pain? How can we prepare the ground for belief in Divine Providence, a life of hope, a life of knowledge of God as Love, from Whom all love takes its origin, Who has "loved us first" (1 Jn. 4:19)—vocation of responding to God's love, by loving as He loved (Jn. 13:34; 15:9-13) and extending His crucified and yet victorious love, a love victorious *while* crucified, into the world (Col. 1:24)?

Strange errors have been held in the name of Christianity. Any imbalance, if consistently held, will destroy the heart of faith, which will always have to be a *coincidentia oppositorium*, a coming together into a mysterious unity of what seems incompatible—three Persons, one Nature; Someone being true God and true Man; God's infinite power and freedom and man's freedom; sufferings of the innocent, of children, creation groaning "inwardly as we wait for our bodies to be set free" (Rom. 8: 22-23), while Divine Providence with infinite compassion watches over us. How are we to live and believe and hope and love the Creator and man, the crown of creation? How do we unite in our faith "God's everlasting power and deity . . . [seen] in the things He has made" (Rom. 1:20) with the grave disorders among men, now increasingly threatening even nature?

We cannot believe unless we are vividly aware that we were not intended by God to be what we are now. We were created "in holiness and justice, not knowing evil or death" (Credo of Pope Paul VI). Original Sin has changed all this, and the continuation of the Fall in us, through us, in and through *me*, has set man, all men, in profound contradiction to the Creator. We have come into the world without capacity for God, and are helpless without Him. Our sins have aggravated this condition. Realization of these realities is the first requirement if we are to believe in God's compassionate Providence, if we are to hear the call to become instruments of His Providence, channels of His redeeming will.

We must also vividly believe that God interposed Himself into the world to become the target and victim of the totality of man's rebellion. He became vulnerable, by entering His world by Incarnation. He came, and "was in the world that had its being through Him, and the world"—that is, we—"did not know Him" (Jn. 1:10). Yet when He had come we could see—and some *did* see—"His glory, that glory that is His as the only Son of that Father, full of grace and truth" (Jn. 1:14). We must integrate into our faith not only that Jesus Christ was crucified, but that all sins of all men, and above all, *my* sins, tortured and murdered Him, Whom to see is to see the Father (Jn. 14:9). I must see myself in twofold guilt: as co-torturer and co-murderer of Jesus by my sins, as one who has failed to be a "fellow worker with God" (1 Cor. 3:9), ambassador of Christ through whom God wishes to appeal (2 Cor. 5:20)—"neither cold nor hot," to be spit out of God's mouth (Rev. 3:14, 16). My share in causing injustice and suffering may be hidden, but it is large indeed. My failure to alleviate suffering, to carry *my* cross (Mt. 10:38) in expiation, to seek to enter into, and acquire, the mind of Christ, Who emptied Himself to be servant and suffer death on the cross (Phil. 2:1-8)—I do not wish to hear this. I will "listen and listen again, but not understand, see and see again, but not perceive. For the heart of this nation"—*my* heart—"has grown coarse, . . . for fear they [I] should see . . . hear . . . understand . . . and be converted and be healed . . . " (Mt. 13:14:15). I fear conversion and redemption—fear the cross, I, follower of the Crucified, baptized into Christ! And yet, He bore our sins (2 Cor. 5:21; 1 Pt. 2:24), that is, He suffered what Sin intends—elimination of truth, justice, holiness, of God, Who as Love is Source of all. But we were redeemed when, on the cross, He remained faithful while we were unfaithful (2 Tim. 2:13; Jn. 12:32).

Living faith does not consist in believing each dogma, with some intellectual ability to reason out interrelations. Living faith involves the blending and mutual illumination of whatever we discover about God and of His ways, which reveal Him. And what we discover, we must see as God's answer to man in his sin, rebellion, mediocrity, in his growing ability to crucify again the Lord Jesus in those whom He loves. Then God's love will begin to be seen as Divine Providence. It is the blending in the Oneness of the Godhead of His infinite power, knowledge and wisdom. It is His patience, since He wants "*nobody* to be lost and *everybody* to be brought to change his ways" (2 Pt. 3:9). It is His manifold compassion as manifested in His dealing with Israel, in Our Lord and in His tears. If to see Jesus is to see the invisible God (Jn. 14:9), Jesus' humility and meekness (Mt. 11:29) blend into God's revelation of Himself. The Beatitudes are descriptions of what it is to be Christlike, what Christ *is*, and thereby they also speak of the Invisible, Triune God. Every word, gesture, situation, stage of life of Jesus Christ are revelations of God. They are further illuminated in the Christlike lives and deaths of vast numbers of saints through the ages. Thus "God shows to men, in a vivid way, His presence and His face in the lives of those companions of ours in the human condition who are more perfectly transformed into the image of Christ" (*Dogmatic Constitution*, 50).

As all we learn about God and retain and allow, through meditation and adoration, to converge into that unfathomable Mystery which God is eternally, Divine Providence becomes the ground of our hope and the magnet of our love. And we, in our pathetic weakness, may actually become instruments of this ever active love, the Providence of Him Who "wants everyone to be saved" (1 Tim. 2:4), Who "has imprisoned all men in their disobedience only to show mercy to all mankind" (Rom. 11:32).

We live by Divine Providence as we learn to adore God by praying *with* and *as* the Church in the Sacred Liturgy; as we place our intelligence, enlightened by faith, in the service of God; as we learn, on Calvary, of the wisdom, of God (1 Cor. 1:17-2:9) and reject the wisdom of men. As we set our hearts "on His kingdom first, and on His holiness" (Mt. 6:33)—learn of, and adore His glory, the Oneness of Power, Wisdom, Love, enveloping us in their mutual service. And in ways that are not ours, we believe that His creative, compassionate, redeeming word "goes forth from [His] mouth; [that] it will not return to [Him] void, but shall do [His] will, achieving the end for which [He] sent it" (Is. 55:11). "Let us be confident, then, in approaching the throne of grace, that we shall have mercy from Him and find grace when we are in need of help" (Heb. 4:16).

Do Not Judge

Do not judge, and you will not be judged; because the judgements you give
are the jugdements you will get, and the amount you measure out
is the amount you will be given. Why do you observe the splinter
in your brother's eye and never notice the plank in your own?
How dare you say to your brother, 'Let me take the splinter
out of your eye,' when all the time there is a plank in your own? Hypocrite!
Take the plank out of your own eye first, and then you will see
clearly enough to take the splinter out of the brother's eye. (7:1-5)

"If there is one of you who has not sinned, let him be the first to throw a stone at her" (Jn. 8:7). The most fearful effect of Original Sin in us is the continuation of that primeval temptation—that we only would have to defy God, and we would discover that His threat of death (Gen. 3:3), of the loss of eternal life, of our union with Him, was mere rhetoric, if not a lie. That we would find that in defying Him, in asserting our autonomy, we will discover that we are like Him, that it is we who could determine what is good and evil (Gen. 3:4-5). It is the continuing temptation to godlessness. And judging, that is, condemning others, is a way of usurping the prerogative of God, Who alone can see the hearts of men. "Man sees the appearance, but the Lord looks into the heart" (1 Sm. 16:7).

We must be careful to understand what sort of judging is wrong. After all, we must judge candidates in a democracy, we must evaluate students, we must hire people—actually, in most human relations we have to judge. But we only know what appears, we do not know the heart. Even our own heart we do not know. What we must avoid is the presumption of knowledge of consciences, how people actually stand before God, their true motives. For in presuming to know men's hearts we level the infinite Mystery which God *is*, we implicitly make ourselves equal to God, or worse, we reduce God to the level of man—He is thought simply to be like a man with vastly extended abilities, a vast computer able to act. It is the temper of positivism—a fatal misconception of the wonder of existence. It is a sort of opting for stupidity, by excluding vast areas of reality from our awareness.

To presume divine functions, to usurp God's place, always implies the enjoyment of the illusions, of the lies that pride produces. It is an at least temporary suspension or rejection of humility, of being a creature, the refusal to be a servant, sinner, child of God. It is again directly yielding to the ancient temptation, liable to arise in us, to "be like God" (Gn. 3:5). To judge is not only an insolent, contemptuous intrusion into the hidden secrets of another's heart, open only to God. It is accompanied by, and rapidly surrendering to, the fascination of an illusion of power not given to man. For all power given to man is always to be used in the service of God, to love where and as God loves, a love mediated by the human heart of Jesus. All authority of men, in the family, in human organizations, in the state and in the Church, must be a service of love, a duty humbly, even reluctantly exercised. To sit in judgement on others' consciences and guilt is to reject God's mercy for one's brother. If this is my attitude, I cannot really want mercy for myself, and soon will no longer see my need of mercy. I have presumptuously fantasized myself into sinlessness, an attribute of the God Whose function I have usurped. Therefore we have the fearful word of St. James: "There will be judgement without mercy for those who have not been merciful themselves; but the merciful need have no fear of judgement" (Jas. 2:13).

It is something entirely different to fear for the salvation of others of whom we know they have done terrible things, whose mentality we fear to be in opposition, in destructive opposition to the "mind of Christ," the mind of unselfishness, service, and readiness to suffer by the hand of others (Phil. 2:5-8). It is the fear and trembling (Phil. 2:12) vicariously assumed on behalf of those who, judging by appearances, may be on the way to destruction and causing destruction thereby. It is a readiness to let oneself be wounded, to "mourn" (Mt. 5:5) as taught in the Beatitudes, it is sharing the vulnerability of Christ, Who was (and is) meek and humble of heart (Mt. 11:29). It is, like and with Christ, to be the target and victim of any opposition to God. It is to "resist evil and conquer it with good" (Rom. 12:21). It is to be "crucified with Christ" (Gal. 2:19), a condition for living no longer with one's own life, "but with the life of Christ Who lives in me" (Gal. 2:20). It is the life of prayer becoming effective through readiness for the cross, for expiation. Then, "the only thing I can boast about is the cross of Our Lord Jesus Christ, through Whom the world is crucified to me, and I to the world" (Gal. 6:14). But to grow into this crucified life, we must vigorously overcome, again and again, the temptation to usurp God's power, the presumption of condemning, whether from rightful indignation or from evil pride. We cannot be followers of Christ crucified if we reject the cross, if we strike back rather than become targets and victims of evil. And if, as is often the case, duty—that is, the demand of charity—requires action, restraint, even the use of force, it is done with sadness, for the good of the offender and the defense of rights. An absolute pacifism as a policy would only be to allow injustice to prevail and hurt the innocent, if it is not simply to escape from critical reality.

There still remains our first task, as taught by Our Lord—"To take the plank out of [our] own eye first." While blind to our own blinding sins we will rationalize ourselves into the most monstrous positions, seek justification among those who think, live and judge likewise. Positions involving nationalism, racism, glorification of selfishness in what is at times called capitalism, a leveling positivism conveniently reducing all morality to custom and to acquired taste—all these and much else can produce and confirm the plank in our eyes. God alone knows the extent of personal guilt involved. He alone can purify the heart (Mt. 15:19) and reduce or shatter the plank and restore sight to the blind. Only if we become beggars and ask pity of the Lord, and that we might see, will the plank in our eyes be removed (Mk. 10:46-52).

If the continued existence of the plank leads to cultivated

hypocrisy, divine violence may remain as the only remedy. Circumstances of life, a great ordeal, a heavy cross can be the cause or condition of an awakening. Continuing success in life, if dependent on continuing blindness, hypocrisy and self-righteousness, should move us to intensify our prayer and willingness to bear one another's failures—the Law of Christ (Gal. 6:2). The harsh indictments of Our Lord should be seen as a last appeal of redeeming love—"Alas for you, blind guides . . . Blind Pharisee! . . . Serpents, brood of vipers" (Mt. 23:13-39 esp. 15, 26, 33). We do not know whether or when His words were heard and brought about conversion.

It is the vocation of a follower of Jesus Christ to become, like Him, the target and victim of sin, while, in patience not even expecting to see the outcome in this life, but in the service of God, in that charity rooted in the obedience of faith and in hope, "wanting nobody to be lost and everybody to be brought to the change of ways" (2 Pt. 3:8-9). But while we remain blind to the plank in our eye, because of the plank, we will only become more entangled in hardness of heart, self-righteousness, pride, illusion and fantasy. If we are successful in life, flattery will only confirm us in our blindness. We will be blind leading the blind and being led by the blind. We will all "fall into a pit" (Mt. 15:14).

We may soon know whether this is not a description of the political and economic life of the affluent "free" countries of the world. Planks in the eyes of leaders in commerce, industry, technological developments and those responsible in governments seem to multiply. And are we certain that the elements of modern life, the growing interdependence and competition, will not produce so many variables that essential functions will get out of control and become unmanageable? And do we dare hope for a morally inspired wisdom of restraint and cooperation in high places? Can progress continue forever, leaving vast numbers of people outside, often being victimized? Is power, blinded by the planks of irresponsibility, vanity, pride, selfishness, callousness, hedonism, lust, exercised without responsibility, is such power not liable to lead to a rushing into self-destruction, as the swine, possessed by the devils "charged down the cliff into the lake and were drowned" (Lk. 8:33)? And even more frightening, "the entire population of the Gerasene territory . . . asked Jesus to leave them" (Lk. 8:33).

We might ask ourselves whether Our Lord's simple injunction, not to judge and to "take the plank out of [our] own eye first" (Mt. 7:1,5) has implications as far-reaching as suggested above. The interrelations between sin and blindness are indeed frightening and we must face the issue. And the only remedy for sin is found in Jesus Christ, Our Savior.

Do Not Profane Sacred Things

Do not give to dogs what is holy; and do not throw
your pearls in front of pigs; or they may trample them
and then turn on you and tear you into pieces. (7:6)

How far reaching is this word of Our Lord? It is a fearful word. Not only that which is holy will be destroyed by the animals. They will tear to pieces those who committed the sacrilege.

We will consider two areas where degradation of what is sacred is all too common, where the word of Our Lord seems to apply prophetically—degradation and the bitter consequences. First, when the Faith, the Church, sacraments, Church offices are used for political, economic or personal advantages, while what is entrusted to the Church is thereby betrayed and desecrated. The second case is the desecration of what is essentially sacred—marriage and sexuality. This is destroying society and alienating people from the Church, for in defense of marriage and sexuality the teaching of the Church "is intolerable language—how could anyone accept it" (Jn. 6:60). The Church's defense will require of her members the conviction that "the wisdom of this world is foolishness to God" (1 Cor. 3:19), that "God's foolishness" (*Humanae vitae*) "is wiser than human wisdom" (1 Cor. 1:25), that we are to follow a "crucified Christ" (1 Cor. 2:2), "even to accepting death, death on a cross" (Phil. 2:8).

They tried to trap Him, giving Him two alternatives, each for Him a betrayal: to give the secular powers (to Caesar) what belongs to God, or to place the secular, "the world"—the ways of which are evil (Jn. 7:7)—at the service of God in the Church (Mt. 21:15-22). There is a great deal of this found in the history of the Church—giving to Caesar what belongs to God in exchange for some advantage, using what belongs to Caesar in the alleged service of God. Again and again there are Church and State aiding each other, not for the sake of God's kingdom, not for the good of people, not for the true advantage of each other, but for questionable if not corrupt advantages.

Throughout history, the Church has been betrayed from within, as the Lord was betrayed by Judas with a kiss (Mt. 26:49-50); what is holy was given to the dogs, and pearls were thrown in front of pigs, to be trampled on. And as predicted here by Our Lord, the powers aided by the Church in their pursuit of injustices turned on the Church and tore her to pieces.

It is one of the great temptations for those holding responsible positions in the Church, in dioceses, parishes, monasteries, convents, universities and schools, to compromise in seeking aid from the world, from government, from business. At first, pride and vanity blind us and we actually persuade ourselves that it is all for the greater honor and glory of God. We see it again and again, fearful illusion, the under-mining of the faith, hope absorbed in success, and charity replaced by the criteria of public relations. But the ultimate meaning of these be-trayals occasionally breaks through, when this sort of crucifixion afflicts a Saint seeking reform: St. John of the Cross, Newman in an almost continual crucifixion once he became a Catholic, Pope Paul VI, Pope John Paul II. Indeed the great Catholic author Romano Guardini must have suffered thus, observing ecclesiastical betrayals in Germany lead-ing to the rise of National Socialism after the barbarisms of World War I. We ought to meditate deeply on his words: "Christ lives on in the Church, but Christ Crucified. One might also venture to suggest that the defects of the Church are His Cross. The entire Being of the mysti-cal Christ— His truth, His holiness, His grace, and His adorable per-son—are nailed to them, as once His physical Body to the wood of the Cross. And he who will have Christ, must take up his cross as well. We cannot separate Him from it. . . . We shall only have the right attitude towards the Church's imperfections when we grasp their purpose. It is perhaps this—they are permitted to crucify our faith, so that we may sincerely seek God and our salvation, not ourselves" (*The Church and the Catholic*, 55).

For the Catholic there is no third way: the gradual weakening of faith causes one to consider what is holy as a useful means to the achievement of illusions offered by pride and vanity, but eventually such a one will be among those torn to pieces by the dogs and pigs, to use the fearful words of Our Lord; and vicariously we all share in the great sadness these betrayals cause. "The more deeply we are formed in Christ, the more deeply we will suffer from the imperfections of the Church" (*The Church and the Catholic*, 54). It is the Apostolate of the hidden expiation through that sadness which allows us to extend the Agony in the Garden into the world. It is a supernatural sadness, tran-scending time and place, as it were a sacramental presence through the members of Him Who "during his life on earth . . . offered up prayers and entreaty, aloud and in silent tears" (Heb. 5:7).

In the "free" Western world, and above all, in the United States, exploitation of sexuality has assumed an all-pervasive dimension. It is not only an undisciplined use of a biological drive, which is nothing new in human history. As the sense of wonder and mystery, the sense of the holiness of life recedes, sexuality is made to fill the void. Its irrational use, separated from the twofold aspect of the marriage act, the unitive aspect as expression of a deep and unselfish love, and the procreative aspect by which man and woman become more deeply integrated into the growth of the human race passing through this life on a common journey to heaven—the irrational selfish and frantic use of sex as the principal content and consolation of life becomes destructive of the values it replaces.

The callous use of the appeal of sexuality in our consumer society also is in destructive contradiction to the true nature of sex. We are dealing with an instrument of Christ extending Himself through the spouses as they are being drawn into the current of divine love, into the sacred reality of the sacrament of marriage. For in marriage the spouses are consecrated to that intimate union, where they are to be Christ to one another. "Our Savior, the spouse of the Church, now encounters Christian spouses through the sacrament of marriage." "Authentic married love is caught into divine love and is directed and enriched by the redemptive power of Christ and the salvific action of the Church." (*Pastoral Constitution*, 48). As, in faith, we are given to perceive the sacredness of the sphere of marriage and of sexuality, the treatment of sexuality in life, in the arts, simply as a means of profit and in advertising will be seen as the sacrilege it is.

Benign acceptance of this by now almost all-pervasive degradation of what is so eminently sacred clearly shows it as what is holy being given to the dogs, as pearls thrown to pigs. We see everywhere what is holy being trampled on. The destruction of the family, of marriage, the untold suffering inflicted on spouses and children is the turning of dogs and pigs against the perpetrators and their innocent victims. The rapidly expanding child-prostitution which Father Ritter and Covenant House are dealing with verify the prophetic words of Our Lord. It is not merely a question of people indulging in some forms of vice, such as drinking excessively, or narcotics. It involves the direct desecration of what in the life of man is so eminently sacred—spousal love and procreation. It is the heart of that mystery which is not only a reflection of the relation of Christ and the Church (Eph. 5:32). It *is* the redeeming extension of Christ into the Church, so that the union that constitutes the Church may be realized and strengthened in spousal love. And this love is to be fruitful in procreation and sanctification of children. As the supreme glory and splendor of marriage, of spousal love and procreation reveal themselves to us, the abominations committed and rationalized even by Catholic teachers can be seen as being described by the words of Jesus Christ we are considering.

St. Paul, in his Second Letter to Timothy, describes the mood of the "last days", asking us "to have nothing to do with people like that", as he described them (2 Tim. 3:1-5). And his description of paganism in the first chapter of His Letter to the Romans (Rom. 1:18-32) is verified and considerably worse in times of Christian blindness and betrayal. They are now "without brains, honor, love or pity . . . and they encourage others to do the same" (Rom. 1:31-32).

"Put God's armor on so as to be able to resist the devil's tactics. For it is not against human enemies that we have to struggle, but against the Sovereignties and the Powers who originate the darkness in this world, the spiritual army of evil in the heavens. That is why you must rely on God's armor, or you will not be able to put up any resistance when the worst happens, or have enough resources to hold your ground" (Eph. 6:10-13).

Effective Prayer

Ask and if will be given to you; search and you will find; knock, and the door will be opened to you. For one who asks always receives; the one who searches always finds; the one who knocks will always have the door opened to him. Is there a man among you who would hand his son a stone when he asked for bread? Or would hand him a snake when he asked for fish? If you, then, who are evil, know how to give your children what is good, how much more will your Father in heaven give good things to those who ask him! (7:7-11)

Later on, at the Last Supper, on the eve of His crucifixion, Our Blessed Lord would speak of the conditions needed for prayer to be heard. After likening Himself to a vine and us to its branches, in living, life-giving union with the vine, He reveals: "If you remain in me and my words remain in you, you may ask what you will and you shall get it" (Jn. 15:7). But what is being asked is to contribute towards bearing much fruit (Jn. 15:8).

The word of Our Lord just given must be heard exactly for what it says and implies, in mutual illumination with other realities revealed. "*If you remain in me*"—if we do not set ourselves against the will of God Who desires "mercy, not sacrifice" (Mt. 9:13; Osee 6:6), Who "wants everyone to be saved" (1 Tim. 2:4). If we remain in Him Who will continue to make His home with us (Jn. 14:23), if we love *where* and *as* God loves us "as ambassadors for Christ" (2 Cor. 5:20), to prepare "a way for the Lord, make his way straight" (Mt. 3:3), then we pray right and will be heard. We have been baptized into the life, "into the name of

the Father, Son and Holy Spirit" (Matt. 28:19; Gal. 3:27), we have become sharers of the divine nature (2 Pt. 1:4). Cut off from Him we "can
do nothing" (Jn. 15:5).

Two facets essential to Christian life and aspirations must be
mentioned and must remain in a light illuminating our life of prayer of
petition. The "fruit" we are to bear belongs exclusively to the order of
the supernatural life, the order of grace, to eternal life, that which pertains to the very purpose of our life—growth in our capacity for God.
But we must also remember that God's thoughts are not our thoughts,
His ways not our ways (Is. 56:8-9), His wisdom not man's wisdom (1
Cor. 1:17-25), that "as the rain and the snow come down from the
heavens and do not return without watering the earth, making it yield
and giving growth to provide seed for the sower and bread for eating, so
the word that goes from my mouth does not return to me empty, without carrying out my will and succeeding in what it was sent to do" (Is.
55:10-11), the mystery of Divine Providence. Nor must we forget that
the prayer of Jesus in the Garden—"if it is possible, let this cup pass me
by"—was not heard. The second prayer, "let it be as you, not I, would
have it" (Mt. 26:39) is always heard *if* meant unconditionally, or at least
to the extent of our readiness for the cross.

"If my words remain in you" (Jn. 15:7)—if the Truth He *is* (Jn.
14:6), the Word of the Father, has fallen on "rich soil" (Matt. 13:23),
finds us in a resonance in faith, in hope, and in that grateful generosity
which grace needs to bring forth charity. Only in this rich soil can we
acquire the "mind of Christ", this readiness to empty ourselves (Phil.
2:5-8) of selfishness to make room for the life of Christ in us (Gal. 2:19-
20) and to share and extend the love of Christ we are *commanded* to
have: "I give you a *new commandment*: love one another; just *as I have
loved you*, you also *must* love one another" (Jn. 13:34). It is the *way* to
become child of God, and it is the perfection, the quality of the child of
God, of the member of Christ by which we become revelations and instruments of Christ. "Try, then, to imitate God, as children of his that
he loves, and follow Christ by loving *as* He loved you" (Eph. 5:1).

The words of Our Lord to remain in us—it is the balanced
blending of His teaching that comes to us in innumerable ways. His
teachings: He as the Truth of God is the Way we must follow; His cross
must become our cross, for "a servant is not greater than his master. If
they persecuted me, they will persecute you too" (Jn. 15:20; read Mt.
10:19-39 on what Christ's followers must expect). We must, longing for
God in faith and hope, realize our inherited and acquired weakness and
sinfulness, recognize the God Who seeks us through Jesus the Good
Shepherd (Jn. 10:14), Who desires the salvation of all (1 Tim. 2:4). We

must acquire the fidelity of God Whose urgent invitation to return permeates the Bible and Liturgy and is crystallized in the Sacrament of Penance, Whose love extends to us in the Sacred Heart of Jesus and envelops us at every moment, however far we may have strayed ("While he", the Prodigal Son, "was still a long way off" Lk. 15:20). We must open ourselves to the blending of the divine attributes that, by Incarnation, have become visible in the Humanity of the Eternal Son, now in the glory of heaven. If He, Jesus the Lord, lives in me, when "I live now not with my own life, but with the life of Christ who lives in me"—provided "I have been crucified with Christ'—(Gal. 2:20 and 19), then I "may ask what [I] will and [I] shall get it" (Jn. 15:7).

What we just attempted to point to is summarized in the word of St. John: "We are quite confident that if we ask him for anything and it is in accordance with his will, he will hear us" (1 Jn. 5:14). We will be heard because we have acquired the mind of Christ, by having emptied ourselves into an ever more perfect capacity of obedience (Phil . 2:5-8), and a growing readiness to bear the burdens of others' failures (Gal. 6:2), in expiation. We are asking in His name (Jn. 14:41), in His spirit. We are beginning to be able to ask with less and less reservations that His will be done. We become more and more able and willing to discern God's will and fulfill it. We are extending His will into the historical moment we live in, extending God's desire which has become our own—ultimately that "everyone be saved" (1 Tm. 2:4)— and thus we are true "ambassadors for Christ" (2 Cor. 5:20). To "ask", to "search", to "knock" is to seek entrance into God's Providence, to become an instrument of His Providence. It is transformation of self-will into God's will. It is to become Church as this was realized perfectly in her who could say without any reservation, "be it done to me according to your word".

The promises, that we will *always* receive, find, have the door opened to us, seem to contradict experience. But if we are to recall that we are going to the One Who is Creator and Savior, "Whose home is in inaccessible light" (1 Tm. 6:16), Whose thoughts are not our thoughts, Whose ways are not our ways, Whose thoughts and ways are as high above ours as the heavens are above the earth, (Is. 55: 8-9), we will not expect to discern His ways. Our hope is not rooted in discovery of the actual ways of Divine Providence, but in boundless trust. "In hope [Abraham] believed against hope, that he should become the father of many nations; as he had been told, 'so shall your descendants be' " (Rom. 4:18). Like Abraham, we must live and hope, ready to "set out without knowing where [we are] going'" (Heb. 11:8). We must not be impatient with God's patience to Whom "a day can mean a thousand years", Who is patient with us all, wanting nobody to be lost and *everybody* to be brought to change his ways." (2 Pt. 3:8-9).

For us, who are to live in faith and in that hope rooted in the revelations *coming to life in faith*—revelations of the loving Providence of God, of our condition, of the "kindness and love of God our Savior for mankind" (Titus 3:4), of His unbreakable fidelity (2 Tm. 2:13))—the mutual illumination and blending of these realities enables us to remain in the darkness of faith, "until, knowing the love of Christ, which is beyond all knowledge, [we] are filled with the utter fullness of God. Glory be to him whose power, working in us, can do infinitely more than we can ask or imagine" (Eph. 3:19-20).

God's answer pertains to the outcome, the attainment of that which lies beyond death and is reached through resurrection. Signs of God's answer to our prayers may be granted in this life. But we must grow in acceptance of the fundamental fact that God's will, His ways are the salvation and growth in holiness of men, of all men. We are to live with this glorious assurance, without presumption, without despair or discouragement.

"How rich are the depths of God—how deep his wisdom and knowledge—and how impossible to penetrate his motives or understand his methods! Who could ever know the mind of the Lord? Who could ever be his counsellor? Who could ever give him anything or lend him anything? All that exists comes from him; all is by him and for him. To him be glory for ever! Amen" (Rom. 11:33-36).

VI

Charity

The Golden Rule

So always treat others as you would like them to treat you;
that is the meaning of the Law and the Prophets. (7:12)

The Golden Rule is not the foundation of all morality, but rather a way of learning its practice. For the believer, morality is to love *because* God has loved us first (1 John 4:19), it is to love *where* God loves and *as* God loves (John 13: 34 and 15:9, and *therefore*, verse 12). It is response to a love which, in passing through the human heart of Jesus, was (and remains) a love maintained *while* rejected. God's love, in Christ Jesus, reaching out to us, teaching us, transforming us, is a love frequently rejected, yet faithful (2 Tm. 2:13). It is a crucifiable and all too often, a crucified love. It is the drawing of all men to Himself, when He was raised up on the cross (John 12: 32), the enveloping of all human beings, from Adam to the end of history, in the redeeming love of God that had become rejectable, "even to accepting death" (Phil. 2:8), in the humanity of the Eternal Son of the Eternal Father.

It is the Father's and the Son's mutual love, the Holy Spirit, sent forth to restore rebellious men to redeemed unity. He, the Holy Spirit is sent by Jesus the Man, Who has now the authority to send, to extend, God's eternal Love to man (John 16:7) to create in us a new heart, that we may "become altogether new creatures" (Gal. 6:15). The human Heart of Jesus "allots" to each one "his own share of grace" (Eph. 4:7). But the creative act of purifying and of drawing into God, to give birth and to nourish the new life, belongs to God, to the divine power shared by the Father, the Son and the Holy Spirit. Ultimately, it is the Father Who sends the Holy Spirit in the name of Jesus —at the request of Jesus, as asked for by His Human Heart. "The Advocate, the Holy Spirit, Whom the Father will send *in my name*"—these are the words of Him Who, as Man, has the authority (Matt. 28:18) to request divine, creative, redeeming, cleansing, transforming action from the Father (John 11:41; 14:26). Jesus *"by his divine power*, gives us all the things that we need for life and for true devotion" (2 Peter 1:3).

To will, *with* God, *like* God, as members of Our Divine Savior Jesus Christ, "everyone to be saved and reach full knowledge of the truth" (1 Tim. 2:4), is love in practice. "All of us, in union with Christ, form one body, and as parts of it belong to each other" (1 Cor. 12:5). our common destiny, beginning with our having been "baptized into Christ, [having] put on Christ" is the root and foundation of all equality, so that "there is neither Jew nor Greek, . . . neither slave nor free, . . . neither male nor female; for [we] are all one in Christ Jesus" (Gal. 3:27-28). And it is to *learn*, to absorb this fundamental equality of destiny, that we must *practice equality* of fundamental rights and claims, to share in God's gifts of the earth and acquire that generosity without which there is no love. The mind of Christ we are to acquire is to share the very generosity that is constitutive of God's own eternal love and life, of the Eternal Son Who, in obedience "did not count equality with God a thing to be grasped, but emptied himself, . . . humbled himself and became obedient unto death, even death on a cross" (Phil. 2:5-8).

We are to be the object of this redeeming love of God, seeking us through the Heart of Jesus (Luke 19:10). Besides, we are, as His members, to become expendable in His task to seek "and save what was lost", to become a sacrifice "for the life of the world" (John 6:51). To learn this love, the necessary readiness for the cross, the Golden Rule—to treat others as we wish to be treated—is a sort of anticipated fruit of a life of love. The Golden Rule, as a sort of law, is a teacher, laying down the criteria, the standard of love. It is learning, in obedience, the *obedience of love*. For love comes to us as *commandment*, and therefore is an *obedience*. We are commanded to love our neighbor as ourselves. What we ought to desire for ourselves in fulfilling God's law we must respect, desire, pray and work for on behalf of our neighbor.

A mysterious dimension is added by the New Commandment given on the eve of Christ's death—to love as he has loved (John 13:34) and will love during His Passion and Crucifixion (Luke 23:34)—to love while being rejected, to love the enemy (Matt. 5:44). To learn to love, to learn what is involved in loving, has become now also to love those who are indifferent or hostile, whom, with or without reason, we would rather ignore or diminish or destroy. We must learn fearlessly to discern what love, the love that has its origin in God, demands. To discern what love requires and to love accordingly demands faith, charity, and, rooted in these, hope for the other. And these three abilities, to believe, to love, to hope, are gifts from God, both as fundamental abilities (virtues, powers) and in their exercise. For "it is God, *for his own loving purpose*, who puts both the will and the action into [us]" (Phil. 2:13).

The Golden Rule is a sort of divine democracy, and as the way to learn by exercising, an anticipation and preparation of the life of charity. Trustingly to obey God's will is both to reduce selfishness and to grow in our capacity for God. Then we will grow in our capacity to labor for God's "own loving purpose." Much in our lives will gradually be seen as opposed to a life by the Golden Rule. This is also true on a vast social scale, for a significant problem in the United States would seem the growing refusal to apply morality in public life. Glib phrases, such as that morality cannot be legislated, easily cover up moral failings. Fearless discussion of the morality of politics must become again a Christian apostolate, while keeping in mind that we are to love (serve) God with our whole mind (Mark 12:30). The use of the intelligence, of our capacity for truth, is a sacred obligation. It must begin in our life of prayer. We are to adore "The Father in spirit and in truth" (John 4:23). The restoration of justice (of right relations between persons, and between men and Him Who is our Creator *and* Savior) on all levels of existence is first a work of intelligence. For the believer there is his intelligence illuminated by faith, impelled by hope, and thus open to charity. He will falter unless rooted first in seeking God's kingdom and His sanctity—to become known and to be shared (Matt. 6:33). For then, and only then, will what is needed be discerned and grasped.

Only when Christian morality begins again to illuminate, judge and inspire human freedom will we have a chance of avoiding catastrophes ever more threatening in the interplay of greed, power, lust, while the means to manipulate are becoming more powerful. The leaven of Christian truths (Matt. 13:33), witnessed to at times by the blood of Christians, becomes the growing responsibility of Christians. Prayer—worship in spirit and in truth—and expiation—to "resist evil and conquer it with good" (Rom. 12:21)—may be all we can do. It is all the prisoners of Gulags and other victims of terrorism, here and elsewhere, can do. But without prayer and expiation, we build on sand. "Rain came down, floods rose, gales blew and struck the house, and it fell" (Matt. 7:27).

We begin to live by the basic equality rooted in our common vocation (that all men are created equal is not self-evident, as Jefferson, in a simpler age, could still maintain). All distinctions cease, as we are all baptized into Christ and have all clothed ourselves in Christ (Gal. 3:27-28). The American ideal, in spite of all failings, of equality and of equality of opportunity, is still a powerful leaven in society. The Golden Rule is its basis. And this Rule is a guideline for living the Commandment of the love of neighbor. And neighbor is he who takes pity on the one wounded—and it makes absolutely no difference whether the wounds derive from someone else or are the consequence of one's own failure or sin (Luke 10:37; see also: Luke 14:25-32, the behavior of the Older Son; Matt. 20:12-16, in the Parable of the Vineyard Laborers).

The implications of the Golden Rule, as the way to live the commandment to love our neighbor, to love where and as God loves, are far-reaching and must be fearlessly reasoned out. Their practice must be independent of "practicality" and human respect. It is to live by

God's wisdom which is foolishness to men (1 Cor. 1:27). And if we expand, as we must, this commandment into loving *as* Christ loved (John 13:34), to love where and when being rejected, to carry the perfection of God—the love of enemies (Matt. 5:48)—into the world, we "must learn to be a fool before [we] really can be wise . . . because the wisdom of this world is foolishness to God" (1 Cor. 3:18).

The Golden Rule is rooted in the love of God for men, guided by that wisdom of His—"the hidden wisdom of God which we teach in our mysteries . . . that God predestined to be for our glory before the ages began" (1 Cor. 2:7). The Golden Rule is the foundation of Christian behavior, it is the *way and method* to learn Christian behavior as it serves as criterion and refinement in discerning the will of God, and it is the perfection of Christian life, the capacity for God He creates in us by filling us with Himself (John 14:23).

In political life, the Golden Rule is the foundation of justice, the extension of love, redeeming love, the measure of equality and the leaven of equality of opportunity. If lived, the Golden Rule is the foundation and the soul of true democracy—humility, formed by faith, by hope for all, and by charity as the Name of God (1 John 4:8,16), enveloping, redeeming and transforming men into His children, into likeness, revelation, member, extension, instrument of Jesus Christ. And of this divine action we are to be forerunners, to prepare the way, to be "a voice that cries in the wilderness" (John 1:23). And in this wilderness, in this world "without hope and without God" (Eph. 2:12) we are to become "innocent and genuine, perfect children of God among a deceitful and underhand brood and [we] will shine in the world like bright stars, because [we] are offering it the word of life" (Phil. 2:14-16). And we will become, by the grace of God, "light in the Lord" (Eph. 5:8), as we learn to "treat others as [we] would like them to treat [us]", while being "massacred daily, and reckoned as sheep for the slaughter", knowing that "these are the trials through which we triumph, by the power of him who loved us" (Rom. 8:36 -37).

The Two Ways

Enter by the narrow gate, since the road that leads to perdition
is wide and spacious, and many take it; but it is a narrow gate
and a hard road that leads to life, and only a few find it. (7:13-14)

The mystery of the ultimate outcome of human life-eternal life, eternal death, heaven or hell—will eternally remain a mystery. It is a mystery of love, of the dreadful possibility of rejecting love in hatred, in cultivated aversion and resentment, of actually frustrating the infinite power of the Creator Whose name is Love, because love makes the Infinite God vulnerable. He Whose name is Love seeks love, and by loving first (1 John 4:19) invites and enables created love to respond. But God's enabling power does not compel, but liberates the preparation for freedom to be exercised by an obedience given in faith and trust. For freedom, a gift of God, is the God-given capacity to receive and accept God, Who is Love, by responding in love to Him Who enables us to do so. For it is God Who "for his own loving purpose . . . puts both the will and the action into [us]" (Phil. 2:13). Our ability to seek and to welcome Him Who is Himself the Giver and the Gift, is in turn God's gift, the enabling gift, which invites us to "put out into the deep" (Luke 5:4). It is the divine call to hope, to trust, to venture, it is invitation to generosity, to become serious about the prayer "thy will be done" in view of the Kingdom to come *to* and *through* me. It is the foolishness of the Cross (1 Cor. 1:22), the losing of one's life for Jesus' sake in order to find it (Matt. 10:39). It is the freedom that comes from poverty of spirit, from detachment, and from counting on the possibility of "persecution in the cause of right," conditions for entering the Kingdom of God (Matt. 5:3,10).

The "narrow gate" the "hard road" that leads to life is the reckless giving up of all self-indulgence which manifests itself in its results enumerated by St. Paul (Gal. 5:19-21). To name but some of these results: "sexual irresponsibility", "feud", "jealousy", "envy". All these enslave and blind us to the truths that alone will make us free. Freedom comes to the disciple of Christ, which we become if we "make [His] word [our] home" (John 8:31). Because this is the way to "seek" and thus to "find" as promised (Matt. 7:7), to "learn the truth and the truth [to] make [us] free" (John 8:32). The blending of seeking and finding makes us receptive, obedient, available to God, makes us "church" or sacrament, extension of Christ Jesus—revelation and instrument of the Lord. God, in answering our prayer, that His Will be done, draws us into his truth sought in faith and hope, and gives us that charity that allows us to respond, to touch and be touched by, His charity. This is freedom—the ability to initiate what He wills, when what *He* wills becomes what we will. When what we hope—in faith, in the light of, and in response to what we believe—when I hope for myself and for others what God wills, and if this hope becomes an active and activating power in charity, then I become free. The truths revealed and realized in faith, these truth becoming the foundation (God's love, promise and power) and goal (eternal life) of hope, now liberate us into that power—charity—by which we are enabled to love where and as God loves.

That unconditional fidelity of God's love (2 Tim. 2:13; Luke 15:20) filling now the Heart of Jesus lets us extend the struggle of Jesus' love, rejected yet faithful on the cross, into the world. His love, maintained while suffering rejection on the cross, prevailing, victorious, and eternalized as His glory and power at the moment of his death, now continues to burn in heaven, as the created vessel of uncreated love. The love which drew all men to Himself on the cross (John, 12:32) now continues, as reward for the victory of this love on Calvary, to draw all men to Himself. Of this love we are to be instruments, preparing the way, crying in the wilderness (Matt. 3:3), clothing and channeling by prayer and action the invisible action of Christ Jesus the Savior.

To become precursor, revelation and instrument, and thereby to continue the work of the Baptist and of the Apostles (Matt. 28:18-20) as Church, is to enter into the narrow gate and to remain on the hard road that leads to life. "Only a few find it", while "the road that leads to perdition is wide", taken by many.

Christians in their individual lives and teachers in their rhetoric often have failed to find a balanced view. Paralyzing fear of eternal damnation or a casual approach to God, so common today in the affluent West—for is not affluence a sign of God's predilection?—both flow from and strengthen false thinking about God. Both destroy hope either by despair or by presumption. We must maintain the tension of hope—a deep realization of helplessness, both inherited and aggravated by my sin, and perhaps more by my sickening mediocrity (Rev. 3:15-16), and the assurance of God's universal love, of his will that "everyone be saved" (1 Tim. 2:4), of God having "imprisoned all men in their own disobedience only to show mercy to all mankind" (Rom. 11:32). This is the mystery of God, Whose name is "Love", Who lives "in accessible light whom . . . no man is able to see" (1 Tim. 6:16), Whose motives and methods are "impossible to penetrate"—"Who could ever know the mind of the Lord?" (Rom. 11:33-35).

May we venture some suggestions for our spiritual life, that may prepare us for a life of hope, for growth in hope, avoiding the paralysis of despair (discouragement) and the escape into presumption, which eventually becomes a sort of practical atheism, and allows us to dispense with the strain of seeking God and with the consequent "danger" of finding Him (as promised). For "it is a fearful thing to fall into the hands of the living God" (Heb. 10:31). Economic and social emancipation, made possible through technologies increasingly available and through techniques of social and psychological manipulation, offer both a promise and a threat (*Pastoral Constitution* 20), but not wisdom. This can only come from above, and is seen as foolishness by man (1 Cor. 1:22-25). It is the Wisdom of the Cross, of crucified Love. We are told to "work for our salvation in fear and trembling" (Phil 2:12).

To live with and in mystery is to contemplate opposites that appear irreconcilable even where the mystery is reflected in human relations. When the Lord prayed that we are to be one as He, the Son, and the Father are one (John 17:22) in mutual indwelling (verse 21-"as you are in me and I am in you"), He "opened up new horizons closed to human reason by implying that there is a certain parallel between the union existing among the divine persons and union of the sons of God in truth and love" (*Pastoral Constitution* 24). Could there be another parallel where it is a matter of rejection of human love, of infidelity, of betrayal, and ways of reconciliation? Could human pardon, human forgiveness, human reconciliation not involve an extremely narrow gate, a hard road for the offender, found by a few—but could the love of the one offended open many gates as life goes on, each one narrow, a road hard to travel for the offender, but opened somewhere again and again along the wide road that leads to perdition? When the bankruptcy of the wide road becomes manifest, when the offender finds himself on a farm "to feed the pigs . . . and would willingly have filled his belly with the husks the pigs were eating" (The Prodigal Son, Luke 15:15-16), would circumstances, or better, God's Providence, not urge him through a narrow gate and unto a hard road? Is this not the way things often seem to happen?

And what about those facing death, from illness or by violence, would they not realize that they have reached a decisive moment, a "narrow gate"? We have the assurance, from Our Lord, that He would draw *all* men to Himself on the cross (John 12:32). And did He not pray the "they", we, are "all to be one" through His and the Father's dwelling in us (John 17:21; 14:23), in redeemed unity? Or are these our considerations merely rationalizing ourselves into a false peace and security? Is it wrong to hope that along the wide road on which so many are travelling to perdition is offered repeatedly in God's Providence, a narrow gate? That if I have rejected several narrow gates through which to leave the wide road, the approach of death would come as a final invitation from the Savior? *He* is the "gate of the sheepfold" (John 10:7), He *is* the "good shepherd . . . who lays down his life for his sheep" (John 10:11). And now it is the Church, Christ in and through His Church, through which he would go "after the missing [sheep] till he found it" (Luke 15:4).

To live with mystery is, to hold on, in faith and gratitude, to the

two, to us incompatible, realities constituting the *one* truth, the *one* reality. God's desire for the salvation of *all* men (1 Tim. 2:4), the Savior
drawing *all* men to Himself on the cross (John 12:32), but then, the
"narrow gate and a hard road" found only by few, and St. Paul continuing to urge us to "work for [our] salvation in fear and trembling"
(Phil. 2:12). These apparent contradictions must blend into that God-
given virtue of hope, which prevents us from discouragement and despair to which some statements could lead us, and which prevents presumption, from which adoration of God in His majesty may protect us.
As we discover more of God's love, and how impossible it is "to penetrate his motives or understand his method" (Rom. 11:33), we will rest
in that adoration of His Providence where mercy and compassion avail
themselves of his infinite power, knowledge and wisdom. We realize
then that the concrete administration of this Providence is given over to
the Sacred Heart of Jesus (Matt. 28:18), "meek and humble" (Matt.
11:29), Who allots to each one of us "his [my] own share of grace"
(Eph. 4:7), and Who "by his divine power" can give us "all the things
that we need for life" (2 Peter 1:3).

To this we add the final and solemn words of the great Dogmatic
Constitution of Vatican II: "The entire body of the faithful pours forth
urgent supplications to the Mother of God and of men that she, who
aided the beginnings of the Church by her prayers, may now, exalted as
she is above all the angels and saints, intercede before her Son in the
fellowship of all the saints, until all families of people, whether they are
honored with the title of Christian or whether they still do not know the
Savior, may be happily gathered together in peace and harmony into
one People of God, for the glory of the Most Holy and Undivided Trinity" (68).

False Prophets

*Beware of false prophets who come to you disguised as sheep
but underneath are ravenous wolves. You will be able tell them
by their fruits. Can people pick grapes from thorns, or figs from thistles? In
the same way, a sound tree produces good fruit but a rotten tree bad fruit.
A sound tree cannot bear bad fruit, nor a rotten tree bear good fruit.
Any tree that does not produce good fruit is cut down and thrown
on the fire. I repeat, you will be able to tell them by their fruit. (7:15-20)*

The history of the Church, up to the present day, has seen a vast
variety of false prophets who "insinuate their own disruptive views and

disown the Master who purchased their freedom." And although St. Peter assures us that "they will destroy themselves very quickly" (2 Peter 2:1), incalculable harm is done. The content of the faith of many becomes distorted and unbalanced. Even if many who accept false teachings may not incur guilt before God, being simply misled, one must fear that some of the appointed shepherds may have become quite guilty by their silence, if not by the atrophy of spiritual, dogmatic or moral discernment caused by neglect through a long period of time. In the United States one may suspect that in addition to a certain failure to love God with one's whole mind (Mark 12:30) there has been at work a certain resentment both with regard to their traditions or with regard to renewal, understandable in a Church of struggling ethnic immigrants and their children. They also may find themselves torn between their loyalty to the Faith and the gross, often ruthless materialism of an expanding and successful America. Some "shepherds" were unprepared for Vatican II, and not equipped to grasp what they read—if they read at all. The cheapening and deterioration of liturgical life, the blindness as to the lack of orthodoxy and the weakening of a Catholic moral sense prepared the ground for the infiltration of falsehood, and worse, of outright stupidity. They accepted slick simplifications, from kindergarten to graduate school, in seminaries and pulpits, which were supplying the content of the faith, of theology, of faith seeking understanding. The Faith disappears from the hearts of men, who are left "without hope and without God" (Eph. 2:12). It is an incredibly sad, apparently inexorable movement towards extinction of the knowledge of God's redeeming love, leaving men orphans in a world where a new cultural and spiritual ice age seems to spread into the minds and hearts of men in areas once Christian.

Much has been written of the sad effects, which in turn became causes of further decline. Profound analysis has been given. But all the faithful are faced with the spiritual task of seeking to remain immune from the influence of false prophets, to develop an ability to sense falsehood, especially when it is apparently sanctioned by Church authorities. The faithful, in their attitude and actions, must remain constructive. Are there considerations that may be helpful in dealing with the most destructive, deceptive and subtle manifestations of the mystery of iniquity? Are there attitudes which make us more vulnerable, or are there reactions that may harm us and others, aggravating the destructions already wrought, by tempting us to a hardening of hearts and minds? How remain humble, strong, clear about issues? When are steps indicated, when does an obligation arise to stand firm, to protect one's children or students or flock, when to speak out against falsehood protected by local authorities, when to seek protection, the saving word from higher authority? How to keep oneself free of presumption or discouragement? How to act from charity, to be both channel and instrument of the love radiating into the world from the Heart of Jesus Christ, the Redeemer of all men? Where does my duty, my task lie?

To gain some perspective: St. Paul tells the Galatians, that false teaching, that "anyone [who] preaches a version of the Good News different from the one [he has] already preached . . . is to be condemned " (Gal. 1:8). The warning of Our Lord, the theme of this meditation, is urgent for every period of the history of the Church. One might even suspect that at times of greater fervor, disputes and errors would become more disturbing. If we see in Vatican II the crowning of the great Catholic renewal that became visible after the fall of Napoleon, a certain impatience to see its promises realized could easily provoke false expectations ready for error, for imbalance. Peter in his zeal remonstrated with the Lord Who had predicted His passion, death and resurrection, only to hear the words spoken to us all if we disregard the pattern of the cross in God's ways: "Get behind me, Satan! You are an obstacle in my path, because the way you think is not God's way but man's" (Matt. 15:21-23). "Methodology", a word so often heard today, may be useful, but we must make "no mistake about it: if anyone of you thinks of himself as wise, in the ordinary sense of the word, then he must learn to be a fool before he really can be wise" (1 Cor. 3:18).

Ours must be the mind of Christ, before we can begin to hope to discern God's will and God's ways, which so often are in redeeming contradiction, at *cross*-purposes, to the ways of the world. For "the world did not know him" (John 1:10). As for us, "a servant is not greater than his master" (John 15:20). To discover the truth, our spirit must be redeemed, transformed by Him Who is the Spirit of truth, the Advocate, Who draws us into unity with Him Who is the Truth, the Life, and, for us, the Way (John 14:6) we are to follow under the conditions laid down by Him (Matt. 10:16-42, esp. verses 34-39). "When the Spirit of truth comes he will lead [us] to the complete truth" (John 16:13).

Conversion of the false prophets, protection of the faithful—actually, protection of the world which must be able to recognize revealed realities—how can one serve both responsibilities? A dreadful dilemma for the true, appointed shepherds! Too often the wisdom of men prevails. God does not want His messengers and rulers to "brawl or shout . . . [nor] break the crushed reed, nor put out the smouldering wick till he has led the truth to victory" (Matt. 12:19-20). And yet the false prophet "is to be condemned" (Gal. 1:8). Much of the right-minded journalism, unobjectionable in reporting and documenting, can be embarrassing in its slick, often superficial, smug tone, lacking compassion, empathy and imagination. What was the God like the "false prophet" might have been taught? Was He the god of the "or else", clearly a projection of human high-handedness, self-righteousness, and brutality? What if one's milieu is infected by poisonous calumnies concerning others, by personal, political, nationalistic distortions? What if Christian family, school, neighborhood fit the description of St. Paul—"we lived then in wickedness and ill will, hating each other and hateful ourselves", while there was no trace of "the kindness and love of God our savior for mankind" (Titus 3:3-4)? What if the "false prophet" for reasons hidden from him, and certainly from us, has come to see in God an overwhelming "other", Who by His infinite, all-pervasive power and knowledge only crushes man's dignity—re-enforced by an atmosphere around him based on this view, so comfortable to authority having lost its vocation of service and obsessed with power and the goal to maintain order and its own power and glory.

Can an attitude free of compassion ever be considered as coming from God? What are the signs that sin—self-righteousness, a merciless joy in condemning, envy of the success of the "false prophet", suppression of guilt for having thought likewise, rationalizing one's hardness of heart or one's guilt for failing to protect the faithful or to correct, to seek conversion of the "false prophet" (Matt. 18:15) who still is my brother—what are the signs that sin is at work in my heart, that my intentions are simply in the service of pride and self-seeking? Tenderness, sympathy, unity of convictions and love, common purpose, being self-effacing, avoiding competition and conceit and to think of other people's interests (summary of Phil. 2:1-4) must be rooted in having acquired the mind of Christ (Phil. 2:5), the readiness to empty oneself by being a servant, and even accepting the cross, death on a cross (Phil. 2:6-8).

If this spirit of Christ, this "mind of Christ" (Phil. 1:5) does not form our attitude towards "false prophets", sustaining both the concern for the protection of the faith of the faithful, and concern, in true love, for the conversion of the "false prophet" however "right-minded" we might be, we will be "simply a gong booming or a cymbal clashing" (1 Cor. 13:1). If we are "without love, [we are] nothing at all"(1 Cor. 13:3).

Poverty of Spirit is the foundation and fruit of a life of charity. It is supported and bears fruit in the other Beatitudes, for these simply describe the mind of Christ, to be sought by us, His followers. But it is above all the third Beatitude—"Blessed those who mourn, they shall be comforted" (Matt. 5:5)—that is essential to prevent our concern from deteriorating into self-righteous indignation, deforming the face of

Christ as it shines forth in the Church. We must be ready for the heavy cross, the true cross of Jesus, to let ourselves be wounded by sin, by falsehood, by seeing and helplessly foreseeing the harm done to others. We must not shirk our share in the tears of Jesus Our Lord—our Shepherds must long, even if they can do nothing but fast and pray (Mark 9:29), "to gather" Jerusalem's, the Church's, God's "children, as the hen gathers her brood under her wings", even when they refused to be gathered (Luke 13:34-35). Our Lord foresaw the destruction of the City and its holy Temple, and He wept. They had not recognized the "opportunity when God offered it" (Luke 19:41-44). We, the faithful, and above all, our Shepherds, must allow ourselves to be "crucified with Christ" (Gal. 2:19) and suffer any of the phases of the Passion from Gethsemane to Calvary. Here we are called to the agony in the garden, when Peter, John and James slept. Is such a sleep unthinkable among the successors of the Apostles?

But the question remains, what is our part, my vocation at the moment when false prophets arise? The real question must be, what is God's will for me? Depending on the degree and extent of my responsibility to protect the faith of others, in prayer, sharing God's desire that "everyone . . . reach full knowledge of the truth" (1 Tim. 2:4), and in expiation, sharing the cross of Jesus, I must seek to discern His will, maintaining a pure sorrow, free from all self-righteousness. We recall the martyrdom of Pope Paul VI as he witnessed the manifold betrayals of Vatican II, the gradual loss of the Church of Holland, the rebellion against *Humanae Vitae*, the crisis in the American Church. How often may Pope Paul VI have been able to say, "even my closest and most trusted friend, who shared my table, rebels against me" (Ps. 41:9). Our Lord, referring to this prophecy now to be fulfilled by Judas, pointed to the betrayal and its prophecy—"so that when it does happen you may believe that I am He" (John 13:19). Would it not seem that the Vicar of Christ was called to be the Vicar of Him Who "suffered outside the gate to sanctify the people with his own blood", and that His Vicar was called "to go to him outside the camp, and share his degradation" (Heb. 13:12-13)?

Yet God's ways of dealing, in His Providence, with "false prophets" vary. Counting in human sin, human weakness and human wisdom which to God, in the light of the total situation, and of our hardness of heart (Matt. 19:8), known to God alone, is foolishness— the Providential ways lie between the crucified Paul VI and the triumphant Innocent III, who so masterfully threw back the heresies of his day. For us, meanwhile, there is left prayer and expiation, and to mourn and weep with Him Who, "during his life on earth offered up prayer

and entreaty, aloud and in silent tears, to the one who had the power to
save him out of death" (Heb. 5:7). And when our understanding, our
faith and hope are tried, we pray in adoration with St. Paul: "How rich
are the depths of God—how deep his wisdom and knowledge—and
how impossible to penetrate his motives or understand his methods!
Who could ever know the mind of the Lord? Who could ever be his
counsellor? Who could ever give him anything or lend him anything?
All that exists comes from him; all is by him and for him. To him be
glory for ever! Amen" (Rom 11:33-36).

The True Disciple

*It is not those who say to me, "Lord, Lord", who will enter the kingdom
of heaven, but the person who does the will of my Father in heaven.
When the day comes many will say to me, "Lord, Lord, did we not
prophesy in your name, cast out demons in your name,
work many miracles in your name?" Then I shall tell them to their faces:
I have never known you; away from me, you evil men! (7:21-23)*

Here is a word of Our Lord that may well fill the heart of the
Christian, of priest, bishop, religious, with "fear and trembling" (Phil.
2:12). Is there not danger that, like the pharisee in the parable who
went to the temple to pray, we may pride ourselves "on being virtuous",
despising everyone else (Luke 18:9)? Like him, we are liable to inform
God from the depth of fantasy and illusion, that we are "not grasping,
unjust, adulterous like the rest of mankind" (nothing less). The cata-
logue of our good deeds is to be recited lest the Almighty and All-
knowing forget—"Almighty"—how nice to have an ally of such power
in our holy wars against pornography, Jews, Liberals, or whatever target
we have graciously chosen to kindle our pride. History, church history,
is full of it. Growing indifference as to the truth of our allegations, conceived in fantasy, becomes a fountain of lies, of deadly and actually
murderous calumnies. "To hate your brother is to be a murderer" (1
John 3:15). The pretensions of right-mindedness, of being on the side of
God becomes certainty, conviction. Delusion will become total and
deeply anchored in self-righteousness. The very religious and self-righteous Pharisees were among those who, "whenever Moses is read,
[have] the veil over their minds" (2 Cor. 3:15). Has baptism, has ordina-
tion removed this danger?

"It is not those who say to me, 'Lord, Lord', who will enter the
kingdom of heaven" (Mt. 7:21). The kingdom of heaven, that is, salva-

tion, belongs to those who do the will of the Father in heaven. The poor in spirit, those persecuted in the cause of right, "theirs is the kingdom of heaven" (Mt. 5:3,10). These are *conditions* for the kingdom; without these dispositions we remain incompatible with God and will have to hear the words, "I have never known you" (Mt. 7:23). We must "know", find a response in Him, be responsive to Him, grasp in faith *His* call, *my* vocation—for the moment, for life—to do the will of Jesus' Father in heaven. "Eternal life is this: to know the Father" . . . and to know Jesus Whom the Father has sent (John 17:3). To be known or loved by God is the cause, the source of redemption, of growth into Christ, of transformation into Christ (1 John 3:2; 2 Cor. 3:18; Rom. 8:29; Eph. 5:14). Only if we let the burning, redemptive, creative, transforming love of the Creator Whose name is Love, only if we let Him, as directed by the Sacred Heart of Jesus, transform us, can we be "known", be loved, by God, "as children of his that he loves". To "imitate God", to "follow Christ by loving as he loved" (Eph. 5:1-2) as we are commanded (John 13:34), is fruit of God's enabling, creative love and source of ability and exercise of love, for He alone "puts both the will and the action" into us (Phil. 2:13).

And yet, in the secret recesses of our anemic hearts we may pray, in a self-congratulatory monologue masquerading as gratitude—too ridiculous to be honored with the name of blasphemy—"God, I thank you that I am not like others". My self-image is confirmed by my admirers ("You will be hated by all men on account of my name"—Mt. 10:22). My popularity reaches to rich and poor alike, as my jovial, reassuring jokes and use of first names show that I love in a truly democratic way. My conversation, as trivial, as shallow as my entire intellectual life, rocks no boat, never offends ("let what you say be simply 'Yes' or 'No'; anything more than this comes from the evil one"—Mt. 5:37). Following the new public relations version of love, I refuse to be judgmental, for I love people, especially those who love me and set the tone for my kind of people ("Why does your master eat with tax collectors and sinners?"—Mt. 9:11). My aesthetic judgments are formed by my likes and dislikes, my moral judgments by the way I feel, especially *after* the act. If I feel good about it, it is moral. If it makes me feel bad, I confess it in general terms that will discourage any decent priest from inquiring further ("From the depth I call to you". "I have my sin constantly in mind, having sinned against none other than you"—Ps. 130:1; 51:33; "Kyrie Eleison", Lord, have mercy!).

The imprecations of Our Lord are among the words that "will not pass away", though "heaven and earth will pass away" (Mark 13:30). Those among us who are successful, respected, popular, should often read Our Lord's words (Mt. 23:13-39; Luke 11:37-54). These words were (and continue to be) the last resort of His love, seeking what is lost (Luke 19:10; 15:4)—me! They are meant for those who "fear they should see with their eyes, hear with their ears, understand with their heart and be converted and be healed" by God (Mt. 13:15). And who is not afraid of salvation in the prime of life, in the intoxication of success, when we are told, unconditionally, that we "cannot be the servant both of God and of money" (Mt. 6:24), that "where [our] treasure is, there will [our] heart be also" (Luke 12:34); that we "must learn to be a fool before [we] really can be wise" (1 Cor. 3:18), that we are to "go to him", who suffered "outside the camp, and share his degradation" (Heb. 13:13) all contained in that losing of our life for His sake necessary to find it (Mt. 10:39), to find or preserve eternal life into which we have been baptized. That is why we let our hearts grow coarse, let our ears become dull of hearing, shutting our eyes (Mt. 13:15).

We need conversion, to order our priorities after the first of the Ten Commandments, as indicated in the other nine commandments, to live by the wisdom of God. Preoccupation with my image or appearance, enhanced by cosmetics, will have to yield to risk being "a thing despised and rejected by men, [being] a man of sorrows and familiar with suffering, a man to make people screen their faces" (Is. 53:3). It risks being hated by the world. "If [we] belonged to the world, the world would love [us] as its own". Conversion, being called, being chosen by God, "withdrew us from the world. Therefore the world hates us". We are to "remember the words [He] said to [us]: A servant is not greater than his master. If they persecuted me, they will persecute you too" (John 15:18-20). And then Our Lord tells us that if we claim him, His favor, His friendship, if we think we have deserved eternal life, He will tell us to our faces: "I have never known you; away from me you evil man!" (Mt. 7:22-23). Our visible achievements, our visible activities avail us nothing, if not done in harmony with God's will (Mt. 7:21), in obedience. Splendid buildings have been erected out of vanity by priests, bishops, popes. How many cathedrals and bishops' residences in Europe are monuments of pride and vanity! It is true, the humble artistry and the sacrifices of the people often transformed these memorials of pride into revelations of Christian spirit, of Christian truths, of Christian sacrifice. Would this be a way of redeeming the times? "This may be a wicked age, but your lives should redeem it" (Eph. 5:16). Ruthless vanity can still produce, by the humble labors and sufferings of others, monuments to the Faith, the faith of the people.

How much pompous rhetoric in the pulpit is designed to calm the scruples of the selfish and rich! It may well prepare the way for the preacher to have to hear the judgment, the declaration of incompatibility between Him Who is the Truth and the preacher who has imprisoned himself in illusion, selfishness, vanity (Rom. 11:32). The wrath of God is now confronted by one who rationalized himself, lied himself into the conviction that he has served God well, Who in turn owes him a reward. The lie is confirmed every time he prays "kyrie eleison", "Lord, have mercy", "forgive us our trespasses". Jesus is no longer one's Savior. Self-righteousness has taken over, and only two possibilities remain. Curiosity may make us ask the Lord, "where do you come from?" I find you interesting. What do you have to offer? "But Jesus made no answer" (Jn. 19:9), as He made no answer to Pilate. Or as a last resort, Our Lord, through the Church seeks to reach us by that fearful realism that foreshadows the words of eternal condemnation, should we die in final impenitence. Whether bishop, priest, parent, or simply fellow-Christian, these are some of the descriptions or judgements of our condition uttered long ago, but still valid: "You have neglected the weightier matters of the Law—justice, mercy, good faith!" (Mt. 23:23) "You are like whitewashed tombs that look handsome on the outside, but inside are full of dead men's bones and every kind of corruption . . . you are full of hypocrisy" (Mt. 23:27-28). "Serpents, brood of vipers, how can you escape being condemned to hell? (Mt. 23:33). "You are like the unmarked tombs that men walk on without knowing it" (Lk. 11:44). Words of the Son of God, words of God! Last resort of love, patience strained to the limit, patience of the God Whose name is Love and Whose infinite power therefore can be defied, even to final hardening; that patience that wants "nobody to be lost and everybody to be brought to change his ways" (2 Pt. 3:9).

How easy "to keep up the outward appearance of religion but [to] have rejected the inner power of it" (2 Tim. 3:5). And is not the history of the Church, in spite of all its glories of sanctity, of its leavening of mankind, its vast armies of hidden saints, so depressing to behold? How true the words of Bossuet: "O damnable faithlessness of those who glory in the name of Christian! Christians bring about their own destruction; the whole Church is bloody with the murder of her children by her children; and as if so many wars and such slaughter were not enough to sanctify our pitiless inhumanity, we rend each other in the same cities, the same houses, under the same roofs, with irreconcilable enmity. We perpetually ask for peace, and we make war on ourselves . . . so far have we forgotten the Gospel, which is a discipline of peace . . . If indeed, O my Saviour, You wished that the holy union of the faithful should be the mark of Your coming, what do all Christians now but proclaim from the housetops that Your Father never sent You, that the

Gospel is a fantasy, and that Your mysteries are so many fables?" And is not this what almost compels so many to be atheists or agnostics? Atheists of deep regret?

And so we pray, hoping that what we pray may become an expression and description of the truth, however far we still are away from it. "God, you know how foolish I have been, my offenses are not hidden from you; but let those who hope in you not blush for me, Yahweh Sabaoth! Let those who seek you not be ashamed of me, God of Israel! It is for you I am putting up with insults that cover me with shame, that make me a stranger to my brothers, and alien to my mother's other sons; zeal for your house devours me, and the insults of those who insult you fall on me" (Ps. 69:5-9).

The Mystery of the Collapse of Faith

Everyone who listens to these words of mine and acts on them will be like a sensible man who built his house on rock. Rain came down, floods rose, gales blew and hurled themselves against that house, and it did not fall: it was founded on rock. But everyone who listens to these words of mine and does not act on them will be like a stupid man who built his house on sand. Rain came down, floods rose, gales blew and struck that house, and it fell; and what a fall it had!" (7:24-27)

Can these words, closing the Sermon on the Mount, give us a key to the fearful confusion that has appeared in the Church since Vatican II? What has happened to the faith of so many? Facile explanations simply will no do. They describe certain symptoms, but no more. Influences, movements, philosophies, new waves of "immorality", schools of thought, new wealth, these and much else may well be accompanying and aggravating symptoms and partial causes. We are seeing and experiencing within the Church destruction, accompanied by signs of outright evil, a sort of collapse—the rise or return to an unusual extent of unredeemed life as described by St. Paul—ignorance, disobedience, being misled and enslaved by different passions and pleasures, living in wickedness and ill-will, hating each other and hateful ourselves (Titus 3:3). It is the Mystery of Iniquity, mystery both in its source and in its goal, in the object of its destructive intent—God Himself, the Word made Flesh, the Church, the Body of Christ, the hearts of men meant for God. The sneering tone of some of the voices of destruction, the contempt for the faithful, the elegant silence of many Shepherds, masters of the slick answer, the extent of lying and of double-talk—it is not only cause of deep, of the deepest possible sadness, but sinister, and pointing to powers and intelligences other than human. "It is not against human enemies that we have to struggle, but against the Sovereignties and the Powers who *originate* the darkness in this world" (Eph. 6:12).

As descriptions in terms of atoms, of molecules, of forces, cannot explain life, the human mind, the music of Mozart, likewise sociological and psychological descriptions, phenomena, what appears and can be described and, at times, be manipulated, engineered, useful as this may be, do not make human life and history intelligible. What seems so plausible as an explanation does not reach what is essentially hidden in the order of freedom and grace. The faith once built on rock, the Rock of Peter, imperceptibly has lost its foundation, which has turned into sand. An ever growing gap between the words of Christ and one's life that ought to be formed by these words, has ground the rock into sand. There has been a loss of a cohesive vision, of the unity of truth—of the realization of being member of Christ, of *being* Church, "part of God's household . . . part of a building that has the apostles and prophets for its foundation, and Christ Jesus himself for its main cornerstone" (Eph. 2:20)—and when the rain came, the floods rose (doubt became the fashion), gales (temptations) blew and struck the house of my faith, "it fell; and what a fall it had!" (Mt. 7:27). Sophistication and sophistry are now instruments of destruction, seeking a home among the varieties of world views, religions, sects, philosophies, among gurus or versions of Marxism and hedonism.

It is true, we may learn much from a variety of philosophies, because they often ask the right questions, the mark of true philosophizing. But the sheer absurdity of so many answers does not help man to cultivate intelligence. May one venture to suggest that within the Church a sort of pastoral disdain, an icy contempt for people, is a signal that the Mystery of Iniquity is at work? That truth, justice, love, have lost their power of binding? That the spirit has become diseased? Could these observations be related to today's sad events in the Church? Are we dealing with mystery, counter-mystery, mystery of deliberate destruction of truth, justice, and love?

We cannot presume to know the distribution of guilt. We cannot judge, that is, presume to know the individual's relation to God. "Do not judge, and you will not be judged" (Mt. 7:1)—for the presumption involved in judging would be a virtual denial of the limitations of man and of the nature of grace, of God's very essence, for His name is Love (1 John 4:8,16).

Nonetheless, consistent atheism has now become possible. With growing bewilderment we see its spread and its effect. Common ground between believers and others disappears, as can be seen in the areas of protecting human life and of irresponsibility meddling with genetics, as if human genetics is part of simple chemistry. Synthetic fuel, synthetic man—the difference has ceased. The levelling, the pretense that the "nothing but" leads to truth, to understanding, that the measurable, the quantitative is the only reality, the only intelligible, extends gradually to all areas of human existence. Contact with reality is lost. Achievements, discoveries, technologies now become deadly weapons. The wisdom of this world, of fallen man, is, however, "foolishness to God" (1 Cor. 3:19). The Holy Spirit no longer finds entrance. Other spirits come into possession, and "the herd charges down the cliff into the lake and is drowned" (Luke 8:33). "Rain came down, floods rose, gales blew and struck the house" built on sand, "and it fell; and what a fall it had!" (Mt. 7:27). Stupidity has conquered. Truth, justice have disappeared. Charity has grown cold (Mt. 24:12). Love and loyalty no longer meet, justice and peace no longer embrace (Ps. 85:10).

There seem to be three areas of blindness within the realm of the Faith. First, our age has lost sight of the fact that man and human relations are no longer what they were originally meant by God to be, but are flawed through the rebellion of our First Parents, through Original Sin. For man was originally "established . . . in holiness and justice, (*Credo of the People of God*, Pope Paul VI), a state "in which man knew neither evil nor death".

Second, there is a refusal or inability to see that the world is *creation*. "Ever since God created the world his everlasting power and deity—however invisible—have been there for the mind to see in the things he has made" (Rom. 1:20). God sustains "the universe by his powerful command" (Heb. 1:3). Nothing can exist, happen, function, without God's creative thought. This is meant when we profess God as "maker of heaven and earth, of all that is seen and unseen" (Creed).

A third area of blindness is to believe that man can regain paradise by projecting it into the future. We can see what is being sacrificed to this strange goal, which the victims—tens of millions, if not more—will never come to enjoy. Rather, "Set your hearts on his kingdom first, and on his righteousness, and all these other things will be given you as well" (Mt. 6:33).

We refer once more to some of the ways by which adherence to reality is being undermined, grinding down the foundation of rock into a foundation of sand. The weakening and disappearance of the truths of revelation may diminish and even destroy the spirit. Truth, justice, love may no longer be seen as standards of thought and action. The human spirit and with it, human relations then become diseased. Religion either becomes distorted or disappears. For a while, a sort of benevolent pragmatism, utilizing values originally derived from Christianity, may guide man, hiding the decay. But under the pressures of circumstances and of the corruption of the spirit the "liberal" position will soon be seen as bankrupt, and the vacuum invites unchecked totalitarianism or chaos. Under the guise of compassion, minds unhampered by truth, justice and charity dismiss the protection of life, of health, of rights as too inconvenient or too expensive. In this way human life becomes something indescribably sad, and the destruction of goodness and of beauty prevail. In the interplay of presumption and despair, the presumption of those in power uses the despair of the many as an instrument to increase and maintain their power divorced from truth, justice and love.

Believers, Christians, Catholics must beware that their faith not be undermined by the three blindnesses we have pointed to above. However, we must also beware of seeing these blindnesses with regard to God's original intention, with regard to the fact of creation and the impossibility of attaining to utopia by man's own effort, as the primary *causes* of the collapses with the Church, of the crisis within Catholicism. The pattern of cause and effect taken from Physics, or from mechanics, cannot be applied to relations among persons. What we have considered are symptoms or secondary causes of these failures. Ultimately the break with God has its root in the *heart* of man (Mt. 15:19). The cause is ultimately sin, rebellion, and the destruction brought about by sin and rebellion spreading its effects. The remedy, Redemption, requires conversion. And this can come only from the creative, transforming, enabling power of God and from a God-given readiness on the part of man. *Our* part is to "set our hearts on his kingdom first, and on his righteousness, and [then] all these other things will be *given* [us] as well" (Mt. 6:33). For it is God Who alone, ``*for his own loving purpose*, . . . puts both the will and the action into [us]" (Phil. 2:13).

Come, Holy Spirit, fill the hearts of Your faithful, and kindle in them *the fire of Your love*.

He Taught Them With Authority

Jesus had now finished what He wanted to say, and His teaching made a deep impression on the people because he taught them with authority, and not like their own scribes." (7:28-29)

Who is it Who made such a deep impression? Who would later say, "I tell you most solemnly, before Abraham ever was I Am" (Jn. 8:58)? Who said, "If you do not believe that I am He, you will die in your sins" (Jn. 8:24)? And "I am He" is, and was then understood by those who heard Him to be nothing less than the Name of God (Ex. 3:14). And Who but God could state that "heaven and earth will pass away, but My words will not pass away" (Mk. 13:31)? Was the impression He made mere fascination with a great orator? Was it the power of personality? Was it the sort of impression that has been made, through history, by great statesmen, great preachers who could convey their own fire, wisdom, learning, clothed in language bent perfectly to that purpose? Or was here One Whose words had creative power, beyond the power to *suggest* ineffable truths? Was it the content of his discourse, uttered in His own name, and not as a messenger only, as were the Prophets of old? Was He really an Epiphany of God, so that the "pure in heart" could "see" the Father?

"To have seen Me is to have seen the Father" (Jn. 14:9). It is not to *conclude*, to infer, that somehow the Father appears in human nature, human word and action. It is to see that Father. In Jesus there was present on earth "God's glory, the glory on the face of Christ" (2 Cor. 4:6). For He *is* "the light of the world" (Jn. 8:12). It is the light, the love, the truth, the glory "that is His as the only Son of the Father, full of grace and truth" (Jn. 1:14)—His glory, the glory of the Word-made-flesh, Who lived among us, Who was seen on earth by those of sufficiently pure heart (Mt. 5:8).

The singular, convincing impression He made was not suggestion, not a "great personality," not a magic effect produced in the hearer. It was—and continues to be—something that cannot be reduced to any other human experience. He did not merely *speak* of "the kindness and love of God Our Savior for mankind" (Ti. 3:4). He *was* this kindness, this love; He *was* the Savior of mankind and man, by the grace of God, is then able to *see* His Godhead, of Which Jesus is the visible image (Col. 1:15).

We have tried to speak of the mystery of the Epiphany of God in Jesus in terms of Holy Scripture: overwhelmingly real, yet mysterious. Of course, the believer knows that the Man Jesus *is* the Eternal Son, the Eternal Word of God, one in substance with the Father and the Holy Spirit. But this belief did not yet exist nor was the impression He made confined to the Jews. We find in the Lord Jesus Christ someone Who in his very being bursts all limitations and comparisons. And so we try to listen to His words. At certain blessed moments we realize his words to be "something alive and active, [cutting] like any double-edged sword but more finely," judging "the secret emotions and thoughts. No created thing can hide from him, everything is uncovered and open to the eyes of the One to Whom we must give account of ourselves" (Heb. 4:12-3). We hear, as they heard, the words of Him "Who is to judge the living and the dead" (2 Tim. 4:1), Who as "God, through Jesus Christ, judges the secrets of mankind" (Rom. 2:16). His teachings are not suggestions, but absolute standards, flawlessly realized in Himself. In Him they are of the essence of God, now translated into God's assumed humanity, the pattern and source of our recognition in faith of these realities, these truths, these demands. The life delineated in the Sermon on the Mount, from the first Beatitude to the rock upon which we must build, describe Him, the Lord Jesus Christ, Whom to see is to see the Father (Jn. 14:9). The sermon is articulation in words of Jesus Himself, of his demands, and thus of the God "Whose home is in inaccessible light, Whom no man has seen and no man is able to see" (1 Tm. 6:16). For to see him is to see the Father.

Now, the glory becomes visible, "the glory that is His as the only Son of the Father, full of grace and truth" (Jn. 1:14). He and His truths are incommensurable with anything that was or happened before He had come, before He appeared—compassion joined to infinite power and thereby able to redeem what He rejected. But He came, He spoke "with authority" (Mt. 7:29), yet "gentle and humble in heart" (Mt. 11:29). It is the Epiphany of One Who is true God and true Man. Thus He was seen in Bethlehem by Mary and Joseph, by the Shepherds and the Wise Men; by the Baptist, as "the Lamb of God that takes away the sins of the world" (Jn. 1:29), that is, vulnerable and yet possessed of the creative power of God demanded by redemption; by the people on the Mount; by those greeting Him as "the Son of David . . . Who comes in the name of the Lord" (Mt. 21:9); by the Roman "centurion, together with the others guarding Jesus." "Truly this was the Son of God" (Mt. 27:54).

"Ever since God created the world His everlasting power and deity—however invisible—have been there for the mind to see in the things He has made" (Rom. 1:20). Knowledge of God's existence is not the result of philosophical reasoning, valid as this is. As soon as we are aware of existence, of our own, of others, of the world, we should *know* that existence, that the world is something willed, word of God, of the gods, meant to say something. God is not yet necessarily known as a benevolent or a threatening power. The world is first seen as a face, a countenance, through which the Divine gazes at us, through which the Divine addresses us. Only after that primary realization of the Formative Power expressing Himself in the existence of things, of the world, in the fact that I am, do we see various aspects of the world. In reality we see the world, things, ourselves only *in* this mystery, *in* the One Whose *word*, Whose utterance the world *is*, a word spoken to man.

If awareness of existence brings with it, as the first "given," awareness of the existence of a formative power and will, so that *what* exists is seen as *willed* by it, should not a similar process of relating to reality be found in the perception of Evil? Could one not have hoped—a hope largely disappointed—that the perception of Evil would be "light" by which all great evil would be intuitively seen as what it was? Could not the faces of the leaders, their language, the hellish tone of their voices, the incredible distortions of truth, the sneering rejection of what is noble, the appeal to what is worst in man—should not evil be perceived, not by deduction or by inference, but directly as a simple contradiction to human existence? And on the opposite pole of reality, should not the Christian Thing, and above all Our Lord, when encountered in His words and actions and the words and actions of those who are Christlike—should not He and His continuing witness and influence be seen as Hope, that existence, that its creative source, *are ultimately good and holy*?

And what, if there begins to be seen in the Lord Jesus Christ that "coincidence of opposites" (*coincidentia oppositorium*) which is the mark of the Divine? What of the helplessness of the Child in Bethlehem, of the Crucified, in Gethsemane (Mt. 26:35-39), of the One to be arrested (Jn. 18:4-12) and yet, manifesting power (Mt. 18:6). Vulnerable, meek, humble, and yet a tower of strength. Apparent contradiction, pointing to God both as immutable in the plenitude of His Being dwelling in Jesus (Col. 1:19), and yet possessing the flexibility, even helplessness, the delicacy, the vulnerability of love, of the Immutable God in His compassionate, merciful Love, which by His infinite power, knowledge and wisdom is that Providence which envelops us. "Yes, as the rain and snow come down from the heavens and do not return without watering the earth, making it yield and giving growth to provide seed for the sower and bread for the eating, so the world that goes from My mouth does not return to Me empty, without carrying out My will and succeeding in what it was sent to do" (Is. 55:10-11). This is the Immutable, Who yet "is being patient with [us] all, wanting nobody to be lost and everybody to be brought to change his ways" (2 Pt. 3:9).

Modern Western man, however, has lost this sense of the *given-ness*—the sacredness of himself and of the world. For us, a fatal conversion has taken place. Cognition, action, making, have been drawn away from this relation to the Sacred, to the Divine. The religious act, if present at all, has become a separate act. Man's activities have become deliberately autonomous, repressing the religious dimension. A re-conversion is called for. Otherwise, our suicidal rush into ever greater autonomy will result in what St. Paul describes so fearfully and so powerfully. "That is why such people are without such excuse: they knew God and yet refused to honor Him as God or to thank Him; instead, they made nonsense out of logic and *their empty heads were darkened*. The more they called themselves philosophers, the more stupid they grew, until they exchanged the glory of the immortal God for a worthless imitation, for the image of mortal man, of birds, of quadrupeds, and reptiles. That is why God left them to their filthy enjoyments and the practices with which they dishonor their own bodies. . . . That is . . . their menfolk have given up natural intercourse to be consumed with passion for each other . . . " (Rom. 1:21-24; 26-27). And do we not see this happen, in our own time and country?

We must hear again the call of the Lord Jesus, "the time has come . . . and the kingdom of God is close at hand. Repent and believe the Good News" (Mk. 1:15).

Then his words, He as Truth and Life, He as Promise or Resurrection, (Jn. 14:6; 11:25), will make a "deep impression" and our faith will come to life. The world will become translucent again, and the "everlasting power and deity of the Creator" will be seen, and the world as created, as realization of God's thought, as willed by God, Who has revealed Himself as Love (1 Jn. 4:8), Who has loved us first (1 Jn. 4:19). "This is the victory over the world—our faith" (1 Jn. 4:19).

The key to this radical conversion is the "folly" of the Sermon on the Mount—and especially of the Beatitudes, of poverty of Spirit. And so we rightly pray: "Out of the depths I cry to You, O Lord! Lord, hear my voice!"